HISTORY OF THE WORLD

Civilizations
of the Middle East

CHERRYTREE BOOKS

A Cherrytree Book

This edition adapted by
A S Publishing

First published by Editoriale Jaca Book s.p.a. Milan
© Editoriale Jaca 1987
First English edition published in United States
by Raintree Publishers
English translation © Raintree Publishers Limited Partnership
Translation by Hess-Inglin Translation Service

This edition first published 1992
by Cherrytree Press Ltd
a subsidiary of
The Chivers Company Ltd
Windsor Bridge Road
Bath, Avon BA2 3AX

Copyright © Cherrytree Press Ltd 1992

British Library Cataloguing in Publication Data
  Civilizations of the Middle East.—(History of the world)
  I. Williams, Brian II. Series
  939.4

  ISBN 0-7451-5162-0

Printed in Hong Kong by Imago Publishing Ltd

CONTENTS

BLACK SEA

Kizil

Lake Tuz

Menderes

Catal Hüyük

Hacilar

Halaf

Mureybet

Ugarit

Ebla

Amorite people

Orontes

Byblos

MEDITERRANEAN SEA

Jericho

BLACK SEA

CASPIAN SEA

TURKEY

Kura

Aras

MEDITERRANEAN SEA

SYRIA

Tigris

AFGHANISTAN

LEBANON

ISRAEL

JORDAN

IRAQ

IRAN

EGYPT

Euphrates

KUWAIT

Nile

SAUDI ARABIA

PAKISTAN

INDIA

Indus

GULF

QATAR

UNITED ARAB EMIRATES

OMAN

GULF OF OMAN

The modern states of the Middle East

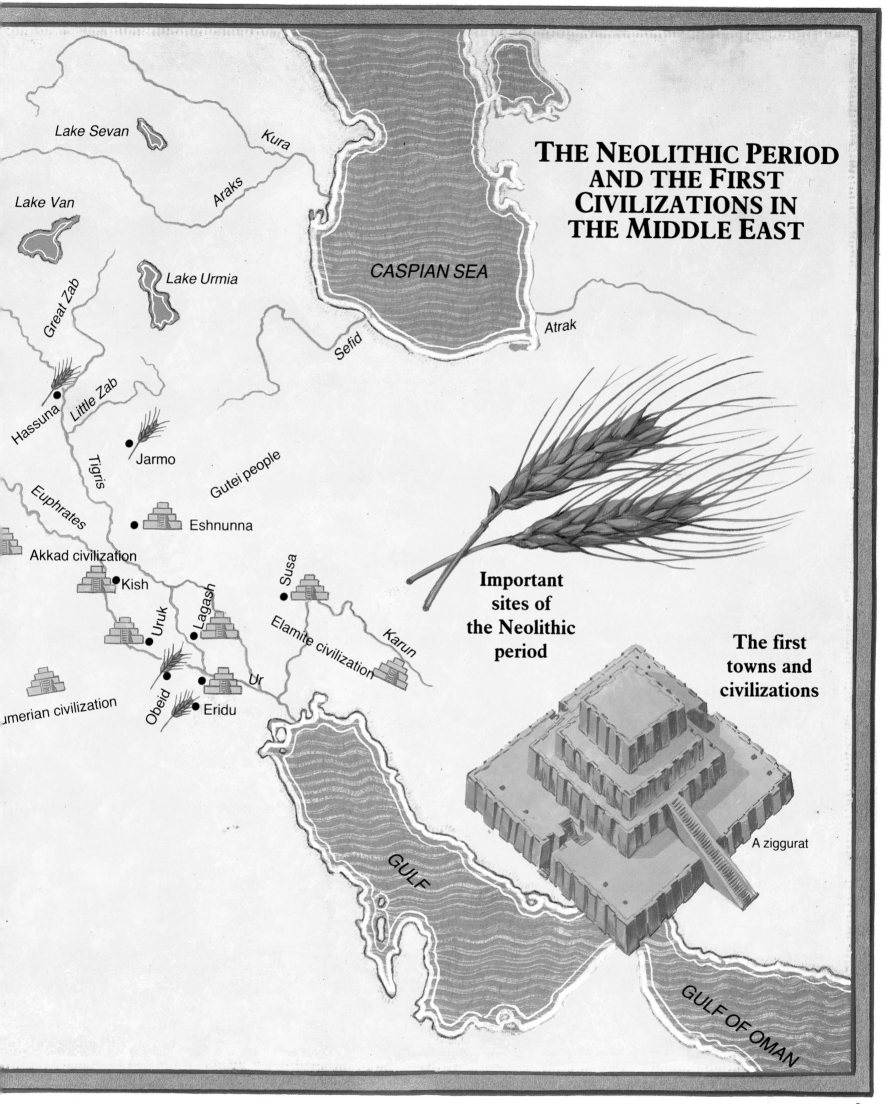

THE NEOLITHIC PERIOD AND THE FIRST CIVILIZATIONS IN THE MIDDLE EAST

Lake Sevan

Kura

Araks

Lake Van

Lake Urmia

CASPIAN SEA

Great Zab

Little Zab

Sefid

Atrak

Hassuna

Tigris

Jarmo

Euphrates

Gutei people

Eshnunna

Akkad civilization

Kish

Susa

Uruk

Lagash

Elamite civilization

Karun

umerian civilization

Obeid

Ur

Eridu

GULF

GULF OF OMAN

Important sites of the Neolithic period

The first towns and civilizations

A ziggurat

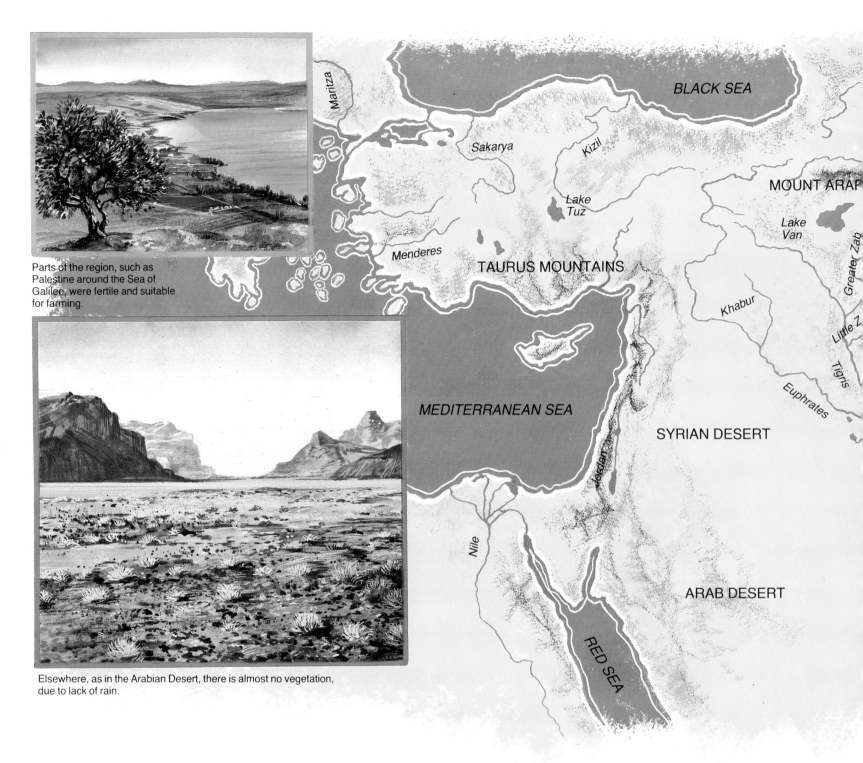

Parts of the region, such as Palestine around the Sea of Galilee, were fertile and suitable for farming.

Elsewhere, as in the Arabian Desert, there is almost no vegetation, due to lack of rain.

THE LANDSCAPE

The Middle East has no exact geographic boundaries. It is a world made up of lands of varying climates and features, with peoples often showing little similarity to one another. The lands are seen as forming one region because of their geographic position; providing a gateway to three continents, Europe, Asia and Africa. Within them, four major environments can be found: 1) the plateaus and the mountain chains, 2) the Mediterranean regions, 3) the valley between the Tigris and Euphrates rivers, and 4) the desert.

Plateaus and Mountains

Nearly all of the western territory is an enormous block of high plateaus and mountain ranges. From this rocky barrier, which extends from Mount Ararat in Turkey to Mount Damavand in Iran, the Zagros Mountains run southward. These mountains form a natural border between Iran and Iraq and extend along the entire eastern coast of the Persian Gulf. In these regions, winters are extremely cold, and summers are dry. There are few natural trade routes and agriculture is difficult.

Mediterranean Regions

The Mediterranean regions also have mountains of great height. But here, the mountains, once covered with forests, alternate with coastal plains and valleys nestled among the

foothills. This is the Levantine Orient: country noted for olive oil and wine. The climate here has fewer extremes. Nature is more generous, and life is easier.

The Valley Between the Tigris and the Euphrates

This great valley bears the Greek name Mesopotamia which means 'between rivers'. Despite its dry climate, this vast region is not a desert thanks to the rivers which run through it: the Tigris (and its tributaries—the Zab, Diyala and Karun rivers) and the Euphrates (into which the Khabur River flows). Here agriculture can be rich, but it is tied to the rhythms of the two rivers. Farmers must

The Karun River, a tributary of the Shatt-al-Arab, follows a winding course through Southern Iran.

Date palms grow along the bank of the Euphrates River in southern Iraq.

adjust to a scarce water supply during the dry season. They must adjust again to an excessive supply in spring when the Tigris and the Euphrates overflow their banks and flood the very flat Mesopotamian plain. To deal with this, Mesopotamia's early settlers, the Sumerians, learned to build canals to control the violent floods and to irrigate the land. Thus, Mesopotamian civilization developed because of the rivers but also in spite of them.

Throughout the world, rivers have played an important part in the progress of civilization. Some examples are the Indus River valley, central Soviet Asia (watered by the Amu Darya), and the Nile delta in Egypt, which was the site of a very early and brilliant civilization. Mesopotamia lacked natural resources; it had few minerals and little timber. Its only plentiful asset was its soil.

Excessive irrigation eventually ruined the rich Mesopotamian soil. Due to insufficient drainage, the lands filled with salt and became sterile. Furthermore, to farm land to the south of this valley required such great effort that it, too, was finally abandoned. The remains of the canals, now filled with sand, are barely distinguishable. Today, this region is no longer flooded, thanks to the construction of great dams. Instead, it is the site of an ever-growing desert, inhabited only by a few nomadic tribes.

In the southern part of this area, gently sloping plains have caused the rivers to branch. These branches then rejoin to form a vast delta. This delta is a swampy zone where people have settled for thousands of years. Their settlements are proof of the human ability to adapt to hostile environments.

The Great Desert

The so-called "fertile crescent" joins the valley of Mesopotamia to the Mediterranean coast and contains the great Syrian-Arabian Desert. The central area of the Middle East is a vast, empty, inhospitable zone. Deserts are interrupted here and there by oases where cities sprang up such as Damascus, Palmyra, Jericho and Isfahan.

7

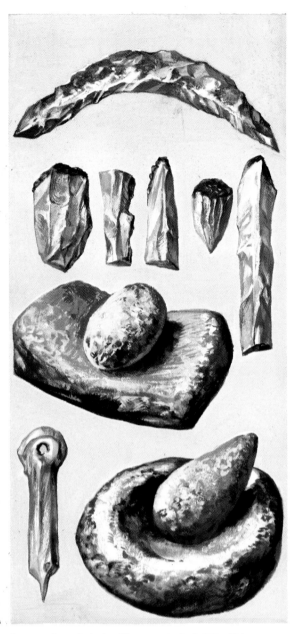

Stone tools, called microliths, were typical of Neolithic culture. These tools were found at Jarmo in Iraq: a scythe for harvesting grain, points and blades for various uses, and a mortar and pestle.

In the fields where wheat and barley grew wild, Neolithic people use wooden-handled flint scythes to harvest the plants, which were much smaller and thinner than the cereal varieties grown by modern farmers of today. The grain could be stored, and so these wild-harvesting people settled wherever wheat and barley grew. Thus, the first permanent settlements appeared. Little by little, people learned to protect the valuable grains against other plants and to save the seeds of the best plants for planting the following year. In this way, agriculture was born.

THE REVOLUTION OF THE NEOLITHIC PERIOD

About 10,000 B.C. there began a period of great change in human history. Until this period, humans had existed as hunters and gatherers of food, strictly tied to available natural resources. Now, humans changed gradually to a farmer-herder life-style and produced their own food. This change was so important to human civilization that it is sometimes called the "Neolithic revolution". The most important aspect of this revolution is that the human species learned to change the surrounding environment. To a growing extent they could control resources, modify certain vegetable and animal species, and so transform their entire social organization.

The Natufian Period

These changes began in the grassy areas at the foot of the mountains inhabited by little bands of hunter-gatherers. Such groups, made up of twenty or thirty people, lived on resources that varied with each new season: fruits, wild cereals, and wild game (especially gazelle). This way of life required frequent migrations across a vast territory. These people are known as Natufians, after Uadi-en-Natuf in Palestine. They occupied the eastern territory from the Nile to the Euphrates between 9000 and 7000 B.C. This period was known as the Natufian period.

Excavations of the Natufian culture have revealed shallow shelters, stone-lined fireplaces, and small pits that may have served as grain bins. These grains were cereals that grew in the surrounding wilderness. Grain had an important advantage over other vegetable pro-

ducts: it could be stored for several months. Because of this, it was no longer necessary to migrate long distances in search of food.

The Discovery of Agriculture and the Rise of Villages

Little by little, Natufian people began to settle wherever wild cereals grew. They learned to recognize the varieties yielding the best harvests, and began to save the seeds of these varieties for planting, so increasing their yield. Villages tended to become permanent wherever these food resources were greatest. Simple shelters were gradually replaced by true houses. These houses were at first round but later rectangular in shape. A new building material appeared: unbaked brick made of mud mixed with straw, roughly shaped by hand.

A reconstruction of a house from 8000 B.C., discovered in the Syrian village of Mureybet. The design is circular. The frame of the house is made of wood. The roof and walls are of clay, stones and straw mixed together. Inside, walls mark off an area for the fireplace, an area for sleeping, and a storage area.
Outside, a flock of sheep and goats grazes.

In addition to plants, humans domesticated some species of animals. They began with those animals that lived in herds, such as sheep, goats and cattle. Gradually, the importance of hunting and the gathering of wild plants diminished. Around 7000 B.C., the main food sources of these people were agriculture and domesticated animals.

Settlements Mean More People

Human settlement was accompanied by a population explosion. This was due, in part, to the fact that migration no longer limited the growth of human groups. As new methods of food production were perfected, single settlements were able to feed populations as large as 150 to 200 people.

Within these communities, however, it was more difficult to settle conflicts than it had been when groups were smaller. When there was a dispute, the village would divide, and a portion of the people would settle elsewhere. Shortly after 7000 B.C., villages began to appear outside the zones where wild cereals had grown originally. By then, people had learned to cultivate wheat and barley in new environments. Within a few centuries, this new way of life had spread throughout the fertile regions of the Near East.

Houses were perfected and architecture progressed. Here two masons construct a wall of sun-baked bricks, binding it with clay.

FROM VILLAGES TO TOWNS

By 6000 B.C., the fertile regions of the Near and Middle East were occupied by farmers. They inhabited areas from which the old Neolithic way of life had disappeared, but they had also settled new territories, especially upon the great Mesopotamian plain. This period marked the height of a culture in which the village was the basis for economic, social and political activity. Village life was to be the breeding ground for a host of inventions, adaptations and social experiments which were to change human life.

This female terracotta figurine clasps a baby in her arms. Found at Hacilar, Turkey, this sculpture dates from the recent Neolithic period (6000 B.C.) and perhaps represents a mother goddess.

The interior of a shrine at Catal Hüyük in Turkey, from approximately 6000 B.C. The walls are richly decorated with pictures and bulls' heads sculpted in gypsum. The people lived by cattle-rearing and agriculture.

Ceramics

The use of clay vessels, which became widespread before 6000 B.C., was one important change. Before this, vessels had been made of wood, skin, wicker or stone. Clay pots provided the ideal means of preserving food. Previously shaped by hand, pottery was soon prepared with more refined techniques. Open-air firing over simple wood fires rapidly gave way to firing in specially constructed ovens, or kilns. Potters could obtain and control ever higher temperatures. Like many other objects of daily life, pots were decorated with painted patterns. Through the evolution of these styles, archaeologists can identify various periods. These periods are named after the localities in which different decorative styles dominated: Hassuna (6000-5500 B.C.), Samarra (around 5000 B.C.), Halaf (5500-4750 B.C.), and Obeid (4750-3750 B.C.).

The Discovery of Irrigation

Agriculture and domesticated animals were important in the development of economic life. As plants were cultivated, they changed greatly from their wild forms. The same was true of animals as they were domesticated. With the development of irrigation, cultivation was able to spread even where there was insufficient rain.

Village Life

Some villages, such as Hacilar in Turkey or Tell es-Sawan in Iraq, were surrounded by circular walls that may have served as fortifications. Although there may have been armed conflicts, nothing suggests that war was constant. Life was relatively peaceful. Houses in these villages had several rooms, usually grouped around a courtyard. Often the inner walls were decorated with pictures, especially

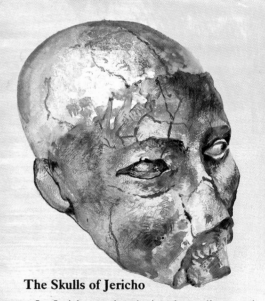

The Skulls of Jericho

In Jericho, archaeologists have discovered human skulls that were removed from their bodies. These skulls are also without their lower jaws. The front part of the skull had been covered in clay plaster, modelled, and painted to resemble a human face. Shells have been placed where eyes once were. Such skulls are from the second phase of the Neolithic period and date back to 7000 B.C. This decoration of skulls may represent a cult of ancestor-worship, or may be evidence of other practices, such as human sacrifice.

The village of Catal Hüyük, reconstructed above, was built on the plateau of Anatolia. Excavations have revealed the existence of more layers. The most ancient date back to between 7000 and 6000 B.C.; the most recent date to 5700 B.C. The village was divided into distinct quarters, each of which had its own shrine. The houses, built at different levels and positioned back to back with each other, were connected by rooftop terraces. These were linked by wooden ladders.

The use of ceramic vessels spread throughout the Middle East about 6000 B.C. The top three decorated ceramic vases are from the Hassuna period; the one at the bottom is from the Samarra period.

when the buildings were used for religious purposes. At Catal Hüyük, in Turkey, frescos and clay reliefs still cover the shrine walls. These works of art reveal the richness of ancient mythology: heads of bulls, sculpted leopards and hunting scenes.

The dead were buried beneath the houses along with offerings and personal objects. Numerous clay or stone figurines, such as the "mother goddess" of Hacilar, are the only evidence of religious beliefs. These objects indicate that the people felt strongly about the earth's fertility, hunting and the cult of ancestors. Apart from family observances, it is probable that the whole population united for collective rituals.

Shortly after 5000 B.C., the first copper objects appeared. Copper (which can be hammered when cold) had been used in a crude state for quite some time, and sometimes it had been beaten into small utensils and ornaments. Now the refinement and casting of copper was to benefit from an awareness of the power of heat controlled in a kiln, a knowledge

already applied in ovens to fire clay. The primitive smiths, like the potters, became more specialized and traded their products and services for food produced by the farmers. In

this way, social relationships among community members became more complex. From small farming settlements, civilization moved on towards the first cities.

This map shows some of the most famous sites in the prehistory of the Middle East.

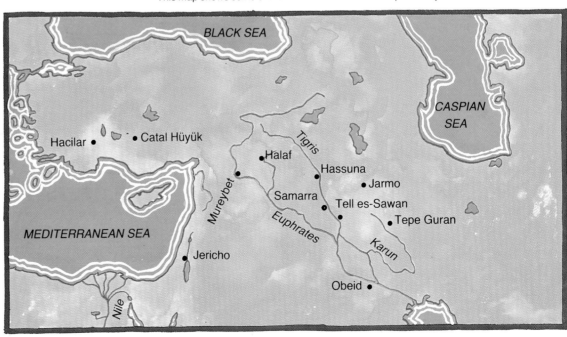

11

Obeidian pottery had detailed, extremely varied decorations. These became less elaborate towards the end of the period. There were only a few pot styles, each functional.

Clay figures of humans dating from 4000 B.C. were found at Ur and Eridu. The facial features of sculptures look somewhat reptilian. The bumps upon the chests may represent some kind of personal adornment.

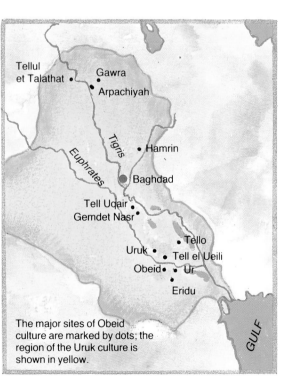

Tellul et Talathat •
Gawra •
Arpachiyah •
Tigris
Euphrates
• Hamrin
● Baghdad
Tell Uqair •
Gemdet Nasr •
Uruk •
• Tello
• Tell el Ueili
Obeid • • Ur
Eridu •
GULF

The major sites of Obeid culture are marked by dots; the region of the Uruk culture is shown in yellow.

The Obeidian village of Gawra. A potter shapes clay vessels, while other people winnow grain from chaff, throwing the grain into the air upon woven mats. In the background a herd of pigs returns from the fields.

OBEID CULTURE

Influence and Subsistence

At first sight, Obeid culture appears unimpressive. But it was here that a long evolutionary process began, culminating two thousand years later with the rise of the Sumerian civilization. This culture lasted throughout the fifth millennium B.C., but very little is actually known about it except its last phases. The Obeid influence reached as far as Syria to the north, but the southern culture emerged as the more innovative, as if the hostile environment had pushed humanity to adopt original solutions.

The soil of southern Mesopotamia is fertile only if it is irrigated. The Obeid civilization was able to expand from its origins close to the Tigris and Euphrates rivers into the interior only after learning to control water supplies.

With water, cereals could be cultivated. Cereals, as noted earlier, had become important because grain could be stored long after the harvest. However, nothing is known of the agricultural techniques that were used. Domesticated animals were important, especially pigs and oxen. In the north, sheep and goats predominated. Fishing was also highly developed in the south.

A plan of an Obeid dwelling.

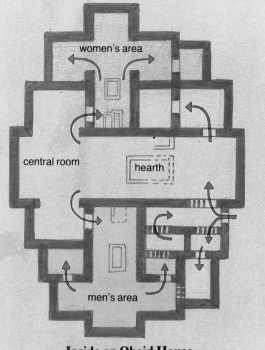

women's area

central room

hearth

men's area

Inside an Obeid House

This private dwelling is reconstructed from remains found at excavations at Kheit Qasim in Hamrin. The plan shows that the house had three distinct sections. The first section included a large space farthest from the single entrance. This was the most private part of the house, where men and women could retire to their own separate quarters. In the diagram, the women's area is shown in pink; the men's area is in green. The second section was a series of connected rooms that were either corridors (such as the entrance atrium and the staircase which led to the roof) or the servants' rooms. The great central room, with its central hearth, was situated between the private apartments and the outside. This room was the heart of the house. It served as a welcoming area, as a passageway to the rest of the building, and as a meeting place for all family members, where daily activities took place.

Pottery

Since their country lacked resources, the Obeidians were forced to make maximum use of what there was. The best raw material to hand was clay. Clay was the best construction material, rivalled only by reeds.

Clay was also the material used most often in making utensils for everyday life. These objects ranged from handmade ceramics ornamented with geometric patterns to objects used in fishing (scales), weaving (spindles, loom weights), tools used to harvest plants (scythes), ornaments for dress (beads and bangles), and religious objects (figurines). Other than clay, the people of this civilization had very little available to them. They were forced to go elsewhere to find other materials that were very rare or nonexistent in their own territory.

Houses

All of the Obeid villages discovered through archaeological excavations are in central or northern Mesopotamia. Each village included a small number of independent dwellings. All were built to the same design, and each was large enough to hold a family of ten people. In contrast, houses in the south (at Eridu, Uruk and Tell Uqair) were larger and more decorated. For many years, these buildings were believed to be temples.

Graves

The only remains which could be connected to religious life are some small statues of animals and human beings. These may have been used in rituals. Burial customs tell little about the culture. Adults were usually buried in cemeteries near their homes, while the children were buried under the floors of houses. Items found in graves included urns full of food and drink and jewellery.

Specialization and Privilege

In the Obeid society it seems that work was allocated according to skill. Some individuals specialized in technical crafts that required an apprenticeship (pottery, flint cutting). Long-distance trade was not yet highly developed, and technology was in its early stages. Luxury objects did not exist, and funeral practices were rather simple, indicating a society that was uncomplicated. The architecture seems to indicate, however, that in the south, around 4000 B.C., a category of privileged people was emerging. Through the storing of cereals, the control of irrigation networks and the monopolization of trade, this privileged group of people was able to extend its power.

Across top: The walls of Habuba-Kabira (Syria). The great Urukian cities were surrounded by walls that served as barriers between a secure society and a hostile world. *Above:* The temple of Tell Uqair, like many important sites, had a great, richly decorated building built on top of a high terrace. These were either temples or the houses of community leaders.

URUK CULTURE: THE BIRTH OF CITIES

The culture of Uruk-Gemdet Nasr (see map page 12) was thriving by 3000 B.C. It was derived from the Obeidian culture of southern Mesopotamia. The most ancient periods of this culture, ancient and middle Uruk, are little understood, but the signs of social change were already apparent. Painted pottery gave way to new undecorated forms. Perhaps painting was considered a waste of time in an economy increasingly concerned with production. But more probably, the disappearance of certain social values was accompanied by the disappearance of those patterns that were their symbols. Burial customs also changed. Practices which had been standard before were replaced by more varied customs, and burial objects began to reflect the social status of the dead. Unfortunately, these bits of evidence are scarce. Even when information available from the earliest periods is compared with evidence from later periods (such as Uruk and Gemdet Nasr), the causes of such changes remain uncertain.

The Aristocracy

In this epoch, southern Mesopotamia was broken into small kingdoms, each with at least one city of great size. These cities were protected by walls and governed by aristocratic dynasties. Rich and powerful, this elite class lived in luxury, commissioning finely crafted precious objects from artisans and organizing great banquets. The remains of such occasions have been found in heaps of crude clay pottery, mass-produced for the banquet. This aristocratic group also built

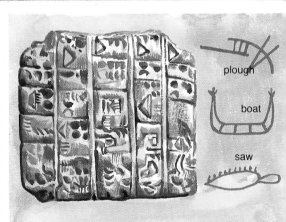

The Alphabet

This ancient clay tablet is from Gemdet Nasr. An increasingly complex economy called for a system of record-keeping. The people of Uruk invented a writing system. Simple sales records from about 3000 B.C. are the earliest evidence of this alphabet. Although the workers who made the records understood them, the script has not been deciphered. The writing system was not able to record all the details of the spoken language. Some of the signs scratched into the clay with a stylus are drawings of recognizable objects. Others are figures that undoubtedly are symbolic.

A basalt stele from Uruk shows a lion hunt. The stele dates from between 4000 and 3000 B.C.

Cylindrical clay seals such as this one from Gemdet Nasr were used by Urukian administrators as official signatures.

Above, right: Some seals from about 3000 B.C. reproduce illustrations of reed buildings from the late Urukian period, similar to huts made by modern inhabitants of the southern swamps of Iraq. *Above, left*, is the Hall of the Pillar Temple at Uruk. The walls and colonnades of this enormous building were decorated with little cones of tinted clay or stone, arranged in geometric patterns.

luxurious residences. Sometimes, as in Uruk, they built giant complexes combining temples, palaces and embellished courtyards unlike any before or since.

The aristocracy controlled all agricultural production (the land, those who farmed it and the irrigation network) and all long-distance commerce. For the supply of raw materials, which the south lacked, colonies were created in Syria to the north, and fortresses were built to protect the principal trade routes. The elite class controlled all systems of distribution, especially those for luxury goods.

Religion and Art

During this time, religion underwent some important changes. Divine personalities became more distinct, and the world of the divinities became organized. The divine world was now a model of the human world. The king became the gods' representative on earth. It was his responsibility to see that the gods' laws were respected and that order (or culture, symbolized by a walled city) should triumph over chaos (or nature, symbolized by wild beasts, nomads, or foreigners).

This new religious viewpoint also influenced art. What might be called propagandistic art appeared in this epoch. This art, which included three-dimensional sculpture, and bas-relief, depicted the king symbolically assuring society's security and prosperity. The end of the fourth millennium thus saw one of the most innovative ages in Mesopotamian history. In all fields, an enthusiasm for invention was displayed. With the Sumerian epoch, however, expansionism led to conflict among neighbouring cities. For a long time, war absorbed the greater part of the energy of this remarkable civilization.

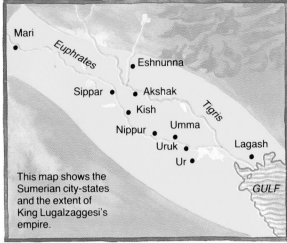

Two wide-eyed statues, apparently praying. Discovered in the temple of the god Abu, at Eshnunna, they date from between 3000 and 2000 B.C. The eyes are encrusted with semi-precious stones called lapis lazuli. The male statue's short skirt ends in a Kaunakes, the common dress of the Sumerians, made of flaps of fur or sheep's wool.

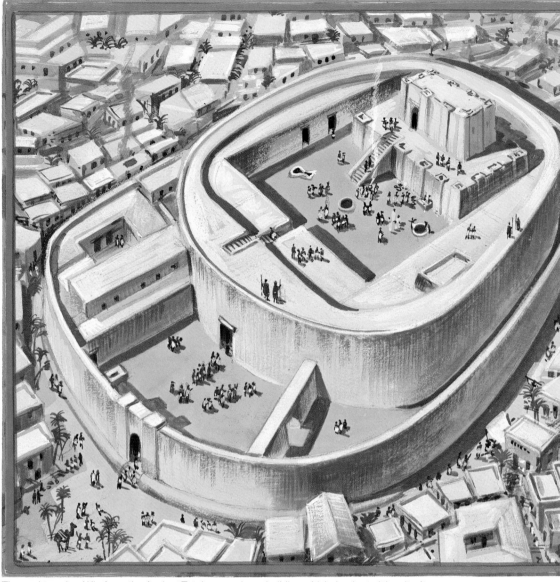

The oval temple of Khafage, the Ancient Tutub, was a huge building which dominated the city. It consisted of three fortified tiers. The lowest level enclosed buildings of the religious cult. The second level contained shops and offices arranged around a courtyard where sacrifices took place. A stairway led to the temple on the highest level.

THE SUMERIANS

Dynastic Rivalries

The third millennium B.C. is marked by a long series of wars between rival Mesopotamian cities. The more powerful cities, such as Kish, Lagash, Umma, Ur and Uruk, conquered smaller neighbouring cities and became small kingdoms. For some time, the city of Kish dominated. Around 2600 B.C., power passed to Ur and Uruk. Even later, power passed to the Lagash dynasty, founded by King Urnanshe. This dynasty reached its height around 2500 B.C. with King Eannatum, who expanded it as far as Mari. Lagash experienced a further glorious period under King Entemena and then declined. Toward 2450 B.C., the reforms of Uru'inimgina, the first Lagash king to concern himself with social justice, weakened the monarchy. The king of Umma, Lugalzaggesi, then easily conquered Lagash, Uruk (which became his

capital), Ur and Kish. He unified the country of the Sumerians for the first time.

About 2700 B.C., the title of "lugal" (king) appeared, together with the first true palace built apart from the temple. However, the king was still the earthly representative for the god of the city. As civil administrator, he oversaw the functioning of the irrigation network to assure the livelihood of the population. As military administrator, he built fortresses or sent men to war. He also undertook the construction of religious buildings and, in ceremonies, played the role of god.

The cities, spurred by local ambitions, remained fiercely independent. Separated by vast expanses of desert and constantly at war, they did not feel that they belonged to common civilization.

Despite their warlike activities, the Sumerians were endowing humanity with a priceless tool for advancing knowledge and civilization namely, writing. Writing was first used by merchants, to identify products and to keep accounts.

Religion

Common religious beliefs were another sign that the populations of various cities belonged to a single civilization. Sumerian culture searched for explanations for the world's mysteries

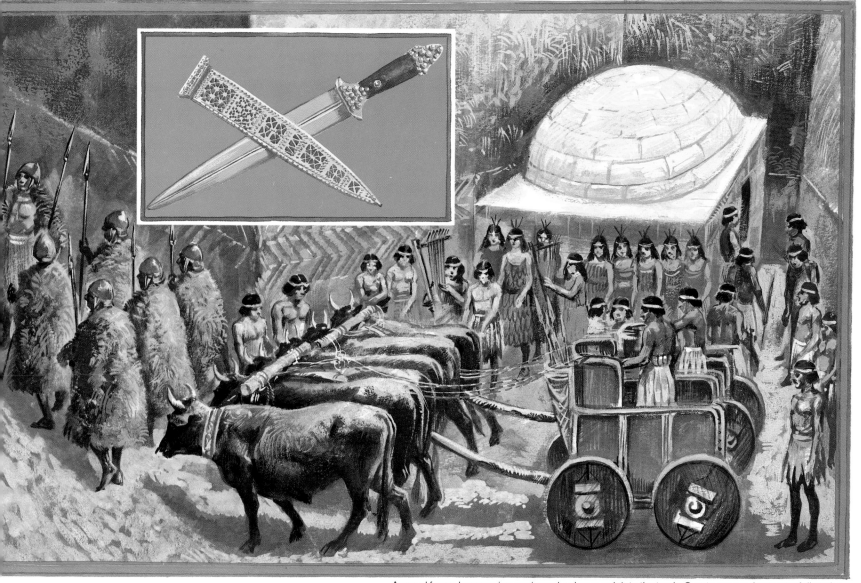

A grand funeral procession carries a dead monarch into the tomb. Courtesans and servants follow the corpse, their own deaths minutes away, accompanied by the sound of lyres. Personal retainers were often buried with the dead, along with carriages and animals. Inset: A golden dagger with lapis lazuli handle and decorated sheath from the royal tombs of Ur (2500 B.C.). These items give an idea of the objects buried with the kings.

ttributing to each divinity a precise function n the universe. Anu was the god of the sky. nlil was the god of air, and Inanna was the eminine divinity. Similar to the mother-oddesses of the Neolithic period, she was esponsible for the greening of the desert after ains. Other gods represented water, the sun, ie moon, war or wisdom. Each city also onoured its own particular god.

he Splendour of the Arts

The Sumerian kings strove to surround iemselves with luxury. This desire encour-ged artistic production and ceremonial rchitecture. For example, the sacred enclo-

sure where the god of the city was worshipped was an imposing structure of many levels. The temple proper was built upon the highest point, to bring humanity closer to divinity. The two great buildings of the temple and the royal palace overshadowed the rest of the city.

The tombs of Ur reveal certain strange Sumerian customs and also the splendid art of their goldsmiths. Kings, queens and princes were buried in the company of courtesans in festive costume. These people followed the royalty into the afterlife by sacrificing them-selves with poison. Members of royalty, ornamented with splendid jewels, were buried along with objects they had used or loved in

life. Helmets, weapons and harnesses were among these items. Highly prized for both jewellery and armour, the combination of gold and lapis lazuli (a semi-precious stone) pro-duced a colourful effect. Mosaics of shells, red limestone and lapis lazuli were used in the decoration of certain objects such as lyres, the most beautiful of which were ornamented with sculpted heads of bulls.

The civilization of the Sumerians attained great prestige before it was conquered by the Semitic king, Sargon I. This occurrence could not have been a violent break with the past since Semitic influence on Sumerian culture had been growing for some time. The result was a fusion of the cultures, encouraged by the shrewd policy of the new dynasty.

Left: The Standard of Ur (2600 B.C.), a panel with encrustations of mother-of-pearl on a backing of lapis lazuli, illustrates the theme of war and peace. The panel provides information concerning Sumerian weapons, carriages and dress.

Akkadian conquests were also opportunities for capturing prisoners who could serve as manual labourers. This illustration, based upon a fragment of a stele from Susa, dates from about 2400 B.C.

The bronze head of an Akkadian king was found at Nineveh and has often been identified as Sargon I. More probably it represents his nephew, Naram-Sin. The sophisticated workmanship of the beard and headdress, the severe features, and proud carriage of the monarch reflect the image that he wished to present: "King of the Universe".

THE AKKADIAN EMPIRE AND SUMER'S REVIVAL

The Akkadian Empire

At the end of the third millennium B.C., the founding of the Akkadian Empire by the Semite Sargon I brought a sudden end to the rivalry among Sumerian cities. Some Semites had long ago abandoned a nomadic life and settled permanently in northern and central Mesopotamia. Some had also settled in the south, where earlier they had mixed with the Sumerian population. Due to their numbers, Semites eventually came to govern in place of the Sumerians. After settling in Mesopotamia, the Sumerians had not received any new immigrants from their homelands, and they had exhausted their strength in war. The Akkadians transferred political authority from the south to the centre of the country, near Kish, in Semitic territory.

An empire of conquerors emerged. In time it included all of Mesopotamia and Elam (Susa). It won complete control as far east as the Oman Sea and the Indus River, and as far west as Asia Minor and the Mediterranean. This policy of expansion permitted the empire to obtain—most often by raiding—timber, stone, metals and other raw materials not found in Mesopotamia.

Little is known about Sargon I and Naram-Sin, his nephew and one of his successors. Many official records of the empire are lost because Akkad, the capital, has never been found. The life and successes of this king are merged with legend because he wished to impose upon his subjects a grandiose image of the sovereign. With the Akkadian Empire came a completely new concept of power. The rather isolated politics of the Sumerian city-states gave way to an empire which proclaimed itself universal and which glorified royal power. This is reflected in the title attributed to Naram-Sin: "King of Four Quarters of the Earth", which was the Sumerian means of conveying "King of the Universe". In spite of their absolute power, the Akkadians tried to respect the Sumerian culture. The Akkadians themselves already followed many Sumerian traditions, especially religious practices.

Ironically, this huge, diversely populated empire was very vulnerable. Rich and powerful, it was highly desirable. Exhausted by military campaigns, weakened by power struggles, constantly ready to fight rebellions in conquered lands, the empire also had to face invasions of nomadic Semitic populations from various surrounding territories. One of these tribes, the Gutans, was responsible for the final fall of the Akkadian Empire around

An Enlightened Prince

This statue depicting Gudea, prince of Lagash, is made of rock called diorite. The statue dates from about 2300 B.C. It is among a series of sculptures that represent the high technical quality of Akkadian art. The imperial ideology of the Akkadians is replaced by the image of an enlightened, humanistic prince, whose face is illuminated by sentiments of piety and wisdom. Lagash had ample means for importing rare and costly materials such as diorite, which probably came from Oman.

200 B.C. After this, the Gutans took control of Mesopotamia.

The Sumerian Revival at Lagash and Ur

During the period of disorder that followed, the Sumerian cities recovered their independence and revived. At this time (around 2150 B.C.), the city of Lagash reached a peak in its history with the rise of the prince Gudea. Gudea exerted his influence throughout the entire Sumerian territory as far as Elam. But not until the foundation of the III Dynasty of Ur around 2100 B.C. by King Ur-Nammu, was effective political authority imposed on the region.

With this dynasty, the Sumerians again exercised control over the affairs of lower Mesopotamia and of the Ur region (later called Chaldea) and conquered a territory at least as large as the Akkadian Empire. This empire, the Neo-Sumerian, lasted a century and had several important consequences. In the military field, it revived Mesopotamian unity. The kings of this dynasty, who were great administrators, tried especially to maintain peace. They tried to reorganize and unify the administration, the legal system (the first known list of laws dates from King Ur-Nammu), the religion, and the economy of the country and the regions under its authority. The trend towards a central administration that had begun in the Akkadian epoch now gained full strength. If the Akkadian Empire was military in character, the III Dynasty of Ur saw the triumph of bureaucracy, which increased the number of clay tablets used in registering, controlling and keeping accounts. The burden of this empire was to be just as heavy as that of Akkadian imperialism.

It was the Elamites who brought an end to the Sumerian Empire. While nomads flooded in from 1950-1750 B.C., the Elamites infiltrated the nearly overwhelmed Sumerian population and absorbed it. The Sumerians vanished, leaving their language to be used for another two thousand years by scholars and priests. This dead language, which was similar to Latin, remains as proof of the ancient origins of civilization.

The ziggurats were among a group of buildings devoted to the Sumerian cult. This one, at Ur, was built by the Sumerian king Ur-Nammu. It was made of unglazed brick faced with fired brick, and measured 43 by 63 metres at its base. Three staircases built against the northeastern face met in a portico between the first and second levels. It is possible that the temple on the highest level rested directly upon the second level. Only the lowest level still stands today.

The yellow section on the map depicts the greatest extent of the Akkadian Empire under Naram-Sin.

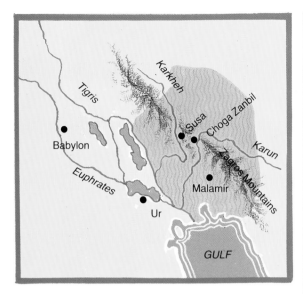

This map shows Elamite territory around 1800 B.C.

One of the principal products of the primitive agricultural Elamite civilization was wheat. It was grown in the plains south of the Karun River. Here farmers are storing the wheat in collective granaries.

Plan view of the ziggurat at Choga Zanbil.

A tablet shows Elamite writing.

SUSA AND ELAM

The plain of Kuzistan was the agricultural heart of the Elamite country. This region, which is southeast of the Tigris, has a harsh climate and lacks temperate seasons between the cold winters and scorching summers. To the west, its communication with Mesopotamia is difficult because of swamps; to the east rises the steep barrier of the Zagros Mountains. Yet here, by 5000 B.C., a flourishing civilization of villages developed, with an economy based on cereal-growing. This civilization was closely related to that of Mesopotamia, but the two became great political and military rivals.

The City of Susa

Elamite society revolved around the capital, Susa. The civilization's economic, political and religious functions were concentrated there.

By 3300 B.C., Susa could already be called a city. It had various temples, an army and an administration that regulated trade. One temple rose from an enormous terrace of raw brick about 10 metres high. This structure was similar to those in Mesopotamia at the time, both in form and in its decorations.

At this time, Susa's influence extended as far to the east as the border of Afghanistan. It seems that the great city controlled all the trade with these distant regions. Susa used this advantage to secure those raw materials (copper and semi-precious stones) that were lacking in its own territory.

Seals and Writing

Seals applied to wet clay were probably the first instruments used by the administration for trade regulation. The seals depicted images

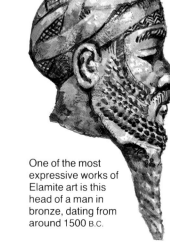

One of the most expressive works of Elamite art is this head of a man in bronze, dating from around 1500 B.C.

Left: A cylindrical seal dating from 800-700 B.C., was found in the temple of Choga Zanbil. A servant waves a flaglike fan while an enthroned figure lifts a chalice to his lips.
Below: The imprint from the same seal is partially reproduced.

An Elamite lady of high rank spins cotton on a spindle, while a maid fans her. The palaces of the Elamite nobles often had vaulted roofs, held up by pillars with arches. This illustration is based upon a bas-relief from Susa dating from 1300-1200 B.C.

This terracotta vase has painted decorations. The lid is made of a bowl, which can also serve as a receptacle. This piece was made around 2500 B.C.

of economic and social life, with many rural scenes in which animals and people are shown. However, a more effective system of management was needed, and so Elamitic script emerged. It was used in business transactions long before it was used for religious texts.

Relations with the Sumerians and the Akkadians

Around 2900 B.C., Susa lost its independence and came under Sumerian control. From the Sumerians, the Elamite civilization adopted cuneiform writing. However, it did not lose its wealth or its role in international commerce, even when it ceded political power to a city whose name is known only from ancient texts.

Around 2350 B.C., the Akkadian king Sargon I made Susa part of his empire with an alliance that was renewed by his successors. No matter who ruled it, Susa never ceased to flourish, even in a politically shaken world. About 2000 B.C. a new royal branch made Susa a capital again and extended its power all the way to the Iranian plateau.

Elam Recovers and Declines Finally

The rebirth of Elam took place in the thirteenth century B.C., with a new dynasty whose greatest ruler, Untash Gal, brought Susa to the height of its power. To beautify the city, he built a completely new capital, Dur Untash (today Choga Zanbil), with a great palace which he later transformed into a huge ziggurat. His successors abandoned this capital to establish themselves at Susa.

In the twelfth century B.C., Elam, which had become a military power, conquered Babylon. But about 1100 B.C., the Babylonian king Nebuchadrezzar I defeated the Elamites. Elam never appeared again as a political force, but its economic prosperity survived. Susa was reborn yet again from its ruins, and the sovereigns of the Achaemenid Empire (550-330 B.C.) made it one of their capitals. But the Elamitic state, which for three thousand years had played the middleman between the Mesopotamian civilizations and the Iranian world, had by then fallen into final decline.

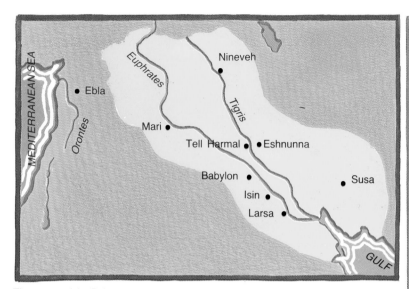

The extent of the Babylonian Empire under Hammurabi.

Right: The construction of palaces encouraged the spread of courtly culture. The sovereigns were entertained by groups of dancers, singers and musicians who often came from far away. These entertainers were regarded as the most precious spoils of war.

HAMMURABI AND THE FIRST BABYLONIAN DYNASTY

For two hundred years after the fall of the III Dynasty of Ur, the balance of power wavered between two cities. They were Isin in central Mesopotamia, and Larsa in the south (not far from Uruk). These cities, the heirs to the rival Sumerian city-states, were in the hands of Amorite dynasties. Both sought control of the small neighbouring Semitic kingdoms.

The Conquest of Larsa

In 1761 B.C. Larsa was overpowered by Babylonian armies led by the Amorite leader Hammurabi (1792-1750 B.C.) With this victory, the Babylonians became masters of the entire Sumerian and Akkadian territory, which they renamed Babylonia. The period between 2000 and 1000 B.C., which marked the rise of the city of Babylon, has come to be called the Ancient Babylonian epoch. The origin of the word *Babylon* is unknown. It is neither Sumerian nor Semitic, but the Semites interpreted it as meaning the "door of god".

While the Babylonian kingdom was concentrating its power, other Amorite kingdoms, such as Ebla and Mari, were rising near the "fertile crescent". This whole area eventually became a centre of diplomatic and commercial trade. The city of Mari, halfway between Mesopotamia and the Mediterranean Sea, was especially prosperous. Having consolidated his

power in Babylon, Hammurabi reunited Mesopotamia through a series of campaigns directed against the area of the Diyala River, Assyria and the Middle Euphrates, where he destroyed the powerful Mari state of King Zimri-Lim. Though the empire was growing weaker as it expanded, Hammurabi was determined to build a nation. He succeeded in inspiring cooperative behaviour in his neighbours rather than dragging his troops into long, wasteful wars.

The Reign of Hammurabi

As the III Dynasty of Ur had done, Hammurabi attempted to centralize his kingdom's administration. To this end, he developed a code of laws, called the Code of Hammurabi. Copies of this collection of laws were sent to all the cities of his kingdom so that the laws could be universally applied.

From the end of the Akkadian Empire, the economic structure of the country experienced major changes. The state tended to lose some of its powers, while those of its people were increased. In a country where agriculture was the sole means of gaining wealth, land management was not always satisfactory, and it was sometimes necessary to cancel the debts of small farmers. Both of these were signs of social unease and general poverty.

The reign of Hammurabi was characterized

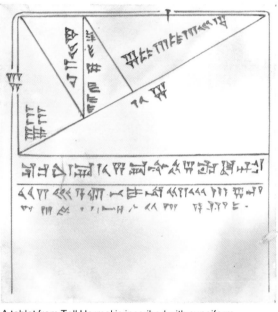

A tablet from Tell Harmal is inscribed with cuneiform writing (an ancient writing form). This tablet contains a geometric proof.

by the rise of the palace as a symbol of royal power. Every ruler built or enlarged his own palace. In the palace of Mari, archaeologists have found murals that reveal the quality of Mesopotamian art. Schools of scribes (letter-writers) were begun outside the palaces and temples, and libraries were built. Here, dictionaries, elaborate mathematical theories and lists of kings were compiled, marking the beginnings of written history. Tablets containing these texts were found at Tell Harmal, near Baghdad.

Science and Letters

Astronomy was one of the major Babylonian

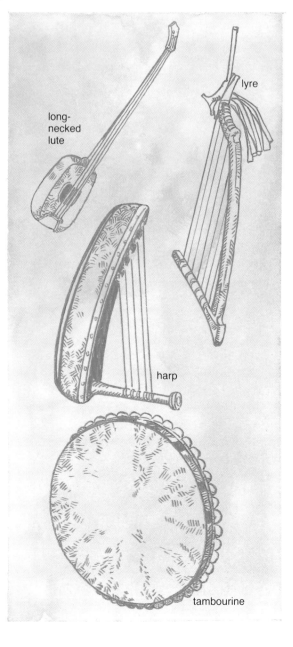

Left: Among stringed instruments, the harp played a very important role in the ancient Sumerian civilization. It later returned to fashion during the first dynasty of Babylon in a much smaller form. The box was clasped against the player's body with the strings positioned vertically, horizontally, or at an angle. The long-necked lute was also played. Its strings were plucked. A variety of percussion instruments including drums, tambourines and sistrums were also played by Babylonian musicians.

inventions, developed initially for divination purposes. From the beginning of Hammurabi's reign, the new calendar consisted of lunar months of twenty-nine to thirty days. These months were divided into seven-day weeks which corresponded to the various phases of the moon. The year, which began in spring, was 354 days long. The language of the period was Babylonian, a local adaptation of Akkadian. The most famous literary work of the Mesopotamian past, the *Epic of Gilgamesh*, was written in this epoch.

The Fall of Babylon

For Babylon, as for the kingdoms of Akkad and the III Dynasty of Ur, maintaining such a powerful empire required gifted kings. Hammurabi faced economic crises and threats from tribes of the Zagros Mountains that had invaded the Mesopotamian plain, particularly the Kassites. After his death in 1750 B.C., these problems brought down the powerful empire. The conquest of the Hittite Mursilis I caused the final fall of Babylon around 1600 B.C. The Hittite conqueror, however, was not the main beneficiary of this victory. He was succeeded by the Kassites, who held power from 1600-1150 B.C. but constantly struggled against Hittites and Assyrians.

Araras, king of the city of Karkemish, in procession, from a large bas-relief (760 B.C.).

A terracotta vase in the form of a lion dates from about 1900 B.C., Kultepe-Kanish.

A bronze sculpture of a god dating from between 1400 and 1100 B.C. was found near Khattusha, the ancient capital of the Hittite Empire.

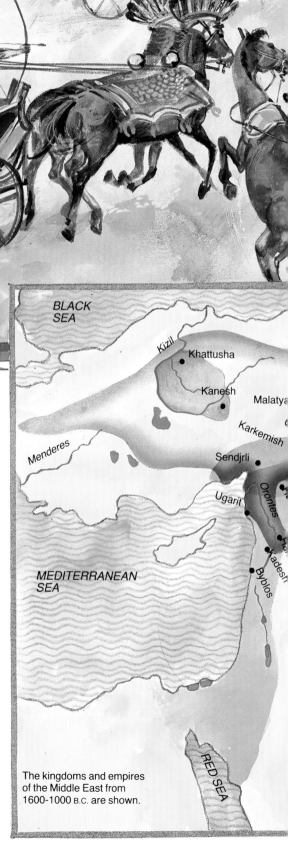

The kingdoms and empires of the Middle East from 1600-1000 B.C. are shown.

HITTITES AND HURRIANS

At the end of the third millennium B.C., great changes occurred in Anatolia, the region of the Middle East from which the Neolithic civilization of Catal Hüyük arose and spread. Indo-European people from the Caucasus settled here between 2300 and 2000 B.C. These invaders took the name of Hittites from the inhabitants of the conquered region, which was called Hatti-Hetei.

The Ancient and New Empires

After centuries of slow integration among the newly arrived peoples and their predecessors, the Ancient Empire was founded around 1860 B.C. and lasted until 1500 B.C. The first great ruler was Anita, who destroyed the ancient capital of Khattusha and built a new capital at Bogazköy. The period of great expansion had its start with the reign of King Labarna (around 1680 B.C.), which was followed by nearly a century of conquests. The army pushed as far as Halpa (Aleppo) in Syria in 1620 B.C. and sacked Babylon in the reign of King Mursilis I, 1595 B.C.

After King Telepinu (1525-1500 B.C.), the empire experienced a century of decline. The second great period of Hittite civilization, known today as the New Empire, began with King Suppiluliuma I in 1380 B.C. Its expansion reached as far southwest as the Aegean Sea. To the southeast, the Hittites defeated the Hurrians under the rule of Mittani.

The new Hittite Empire and the new Egyptian Empire were for some time the two great powers that controlled affairs in the region. The Hittites blocked Egyptian advances toward the Euphrates, and under King Muwatallis II (1315-1290 B.C.), defeated the Egyptian army at Kadesh. After this battle, the Hittites slowly declined in the face of rising Assyrian power to the east and the arrival of the so-called "Sea People" from the west.

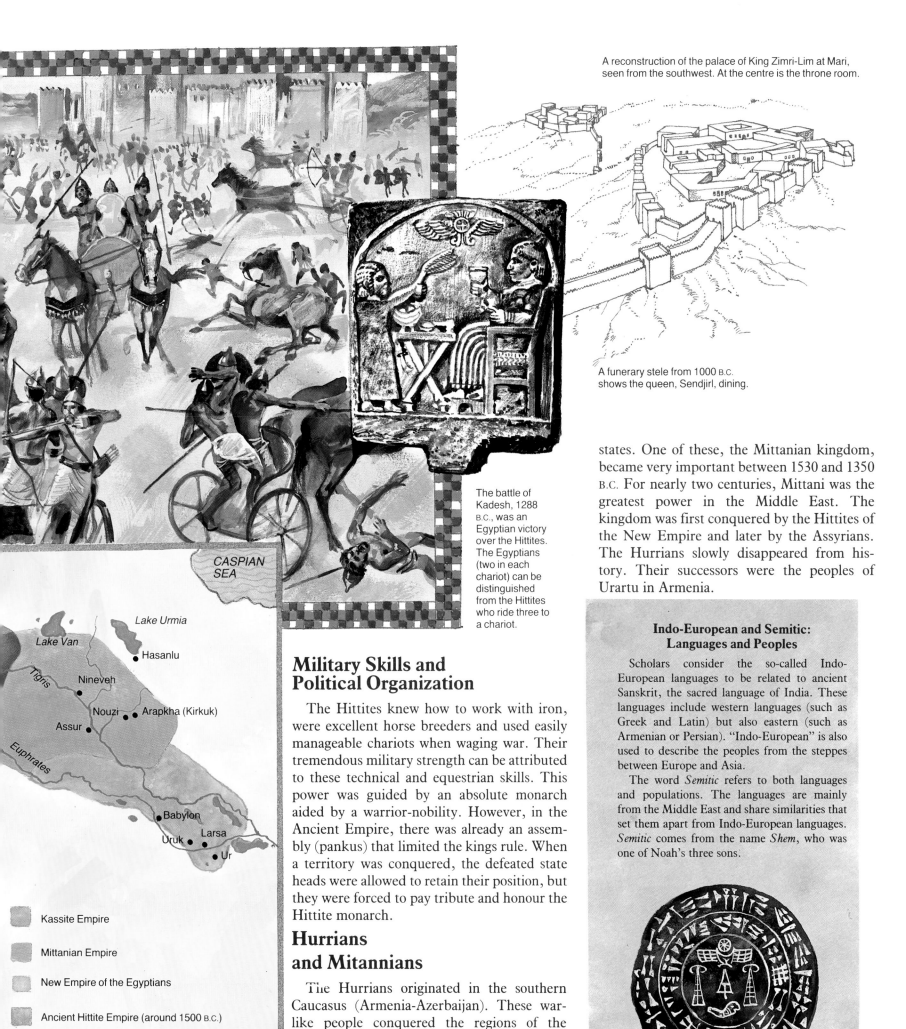

A reconstruction of the palace of King Zimri-Lim at Mari, seen from the southwest. At the centre is the throne room.

A funerary stele from 1000 B.C. shows the queen, Sendjirl, dining.

The battle of Kadesh, 1288 B.C., was an Egyptian victory over the Hittites. The Egyptians (two in each chariot) can be distinguished from the Hittites who ride three to a chariot.

CASPIAN SEA

Lake Urmia

Lake Van

Hasanlu

Nineveh

Tigris

Nouzi

Arapkha (Kirkuk)

Assur

Euphrates

Babylon

Larsa

Uruk

Ur

Kassite Empire

Mittanian Empire

New Empire of the Egyptians

Ancient Hittite Empire (around 1500 B.C.)

New Hittite Empire at the height of its expansion (around 1300 B.C.)

Military Skills and Political Organization

The Hittites knew how to work with iron, were excellent horse breeders and used easily manageable chariots when waging war. Their tremendous military strength can be attributed to these technical and equestrian skills. This power was guided by an absolute monarch aided by a warrior-nobility. However, in the Ancient Empire, there was already an assembly (pankus) that limited the kings rule. When a territory was conquered, the defeated state heads were allowed to retain their position, but they were forced to pay tribute and honour the Hittite monarch.

Hurrians and Mitannians

The Hurrians originated in the southern Caucasus (Armenia-Azerbaijan). These war-like people conquered the regions of the "fertile crescent" between 3000 and 1000 B.C. They were one of the most important and liveliest cultures of the period. Around 1600 B.C., the Hurrians broke into many small

states. One of these, the Mittanian kingdom, became very important between 1530 and 1350 B.C. For nearly two centuries, Mittani was the greatest power in the Middle East. The kingdom was first conquered by the Hittites of the New Empire and later by the Assyrians. The Hurrians slowly disappeared from history. Their successors were the peoples of Urartu in Armenia.

Indo-European and Semitic: Languages and Peoples

Scholars consider the so-called Indo-European languages to be related to ancient Sanskrit, the sacred language of India. These languages include western languages (such as Greek and Latin) but also eastern (such as Armenian or Persian). "Indo-European" is also used to describe the peoples from the steppes between Europe and Asia.

The word *Semitic* refers to both languages and populations. The languages are mainly from the Middle East and share similarities that set them apart from Indo-European languages. *Semitic* comes from the name *Shem*, who was one of Noah's three sons.

An example of cuneiform writing.

Reconstruction of one of the palaces near Khattusha during the twelfth century B.C.

An ancient tablet from Mari contains a list of distributed rations.

Officials at work in one of the archive rooms of the palace at Ebla. The tablets can be seen upon the shelves.

Mari, Ebla, Ugarit and Byblos were situated between the Mediterranean and the basin of the Tigris and Euphrates rivers.

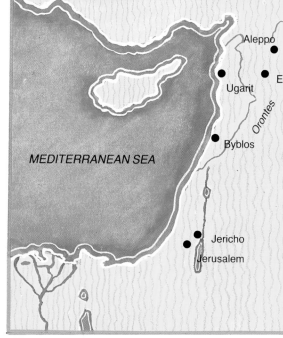

CITIES AMONG THE EMPIRES: MARI, EBLA, UGARIT, BYBLOS

The cities of Mari, Ebla, Ugarit and Byblos were sometimes independent kingdoms and sometimes possessions of a greater empire. These cities had an important role in the trade between the Mediterranean and the Orient. They also influenced the development of literature, with the contribution of two Semitic languages and the invention of an alphabet. As use of this alphabet spread, cuneiform writing, which had been dominant in earlier centuries, was eventually abandoned.

Mari, Crossing-point of the Euphrates

Situated on the middle reaches of the Euphrates River, Mari was an important staging post for trade between the Mediterranean Sea (Syria) and the Persian Gulf (Babylon). Mari became a cultural centre that contributed to the westward spread of writing and art. After two centuries, during which Babylonian influence was extremely strong even in language and literature, the Assyrians of the Ancient Empire conquered the city around 1800 B.C.

Around 1775 B.C., King Zimri-Lim, a descendant of the dynasty which had originally ruled Mari, regained the city. For about fifteen years, Mari again became the centre of a kingdom which stretched through the middle Euphrates region. The city was eventually destroyed by Hammurabi in 1760 B.C.

Ebla, in the Heart of Syria

Closely linked to Mari by commercial and administrative ties was the city of Ebla in northern Syria. The site of Ebla was found in 1968 near Tell Mardikh, 112 kilometres south of Aleppo. The city's archives, discovered in 1975, include about sixteen thousand well-preserved clay tablets. The first urban settlement of this kingdom developed in the third millennium B.C. It was repeatedly destroyed and rebuilt for the next thousand years, attaining its greatest splendour between 2400 and 2000 B.C. A great commercial centre for livestock, fabrics, precious stones and metals, Ebla established relations with many other

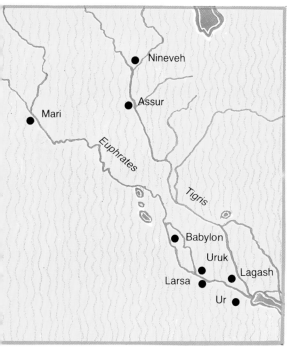

Byblos, the great Phoenician commercial city, viewed from the sea. *In the inset:* Phoenician ships, such as that in the drawing, were used to transport timber.

years. Between 2000 and 1000 B.C., it rose again as an important commercial centre for communications across land and sea. From around 1800 B.C., Ugarit was alternately dependent upon Egypt or Mesopotamia, with only brief periods of independence. The last two centuries in its history are known through the city's own archives and also from Egyptian archives. Between 1210 and 1195 B.C., Ugarit was destroyed, perhaps by an earthquake or more invasions of the Sea People.

Byblos, an Ancient Centre

Byblos is the Greek name of one of the most ancient centres of Phoenician civilization. Its urban development was significant in very early times. From around 2700 B.C., it was alternately dependent upon Egypt and Mesopotamia, and it held great commercial importance. Throughout ancient times, Byblos was coveted by all great powers because of its wealth. Much of this wealth came from the city's commerce in papyrus (*byblos* in Greek). In addition to papyrus production, Byblos's economy revolved around textiles, forestry and seaborne trade. The city was also known for its extremely skilled artisans who did work in gold and ivory. At Byblos, the alphabetical script of Ugarit lost its cuneiform characteristics and acquired those of true writing.

An ivory sculpture from Ugarit (1400 B.C.) depicts the goddess of fertility.

kingdoms in its time. It was also an extraordinary cultural centre. An abundance of administrative, historical, geographic and literary texts have been found.

Ugarit, the Harbour City

Around 7000 B.C., Ugarit was the most important city in northern Syria and was already engaged in trade with Mesopotamia. It later fell into a decline for nearly two thousand

27

THE PHOENICIANS IN SYRIA AND PALESTINE

The name *Phoenician* comes from the Greek word *phoinix*, meaning "red-purple". The Phoenicians acquired this name from a purple dye used in the fabrics they produced. According to the most ancient historical texts, the Phoenicians called themselves *Canaanites*, a Semitic word meaning "land of purple".

The western border of Phoenician territory was the Mediterranean Sea. To the east were the mountains of Lebanon and northern Palestine. The geography of the region influenced the Phoenicians in three important ways. First, it separated them from the peoples who lived in the interior beyond the mountains. Second, the broken coastline kept the Phoenicians from becoming a single political body. It encouraged instead the growth of small city-states. Finally, geography pushed the Phoenicians onto the Mediterranean, since the sea provided their only opportunity for expansion. Skilful mariners, they extended their domain and acquired many colonies.

The history of the Phoenicians began around the thirteenth century B.C. At the time, the Mediterranean coast was a region of great change due to the movement of warlike populations known collectively as Sea People. Mycenae, the Greek state and commercial empire in the eastern Mediterranean, probably also fell as a consequence of these attacks. The Phoenicians took advantage of the situation by seizing their independence. Within a short time, they developed their own trade network.

It is difficult to trace the exact course of Phoenician activities since they left behind very few direct sources of information. What is known of them has come from the historical documents of other peoples, such as the Hebrews. The history of the Phoenicians, or Canaanites, was interwoven with that of the Hebrews. Numerous modern archaeological discoveries of Phoenician colonies are the sole source of direct information about their architecture, art, religion and trade.

Around 1100 B.C., the Assyrians began to raid the Phoenician territory. The Egyptians too raided Phoenician towns to seize much-needed timber.

was Carthage, which soon became a centre of Phoenician culture in the western Mediterranean.

The Phoenicians did a great deal of trading of their agricultural produce (oil, wheat, barley and raisins) and of their crafted goods (vases, statues and ivory carvings). But the most sought-after commodity was timber from the mountain forests of Lebanon. The Phoenicians also traded artefacts and goods obtained from other Mediterranean cultures.

The Greek historian and geographer Herodotus wrote of the interesting way in which the Phoenicians traded with the peoples of the African coast. The Phoenicians would arrange their goods on the shore and go back to their

A stele with the god Baal on a lion, Amrit, fifth century B.C.

The Spread of the Alphabet

One of the major contributions of the Phoenicians was their alphabet, which spread throughout the Mediterranean region. It was the Phoenicians who taught writing with an alphabet to the Greeks. Both peoples later spread its use.

The Religion

The Phoenicians had a polytheistic religion which means they believed in many gods. The main gods were El-Elat and Baal-Baalat. El was called "the Beaming", while Baal was referred to as "the Lord". Baal was more down-to-earth and active than El. He was the

Phoenician towns were situated along the coast.

Colonies and Commerce

The first independent Phoenician colonies were established along the coasts of Spain (Cádiz) and Morocco about 1100 B.C. For the next 250 years, the Phoenicians experienced great prosperity. New towns were founded on the western coast of Spain, on the eastern coast of France, and on the islands of Sardinia, Sicily, Malta, Gozo and Pantelleria. The most famous and wealthy Phoenician colony

ships where they would light a smoky fire. The smoke attracted the Africans, who would come to the shore, examine the goods, deposit a certain amount of gold beside them and retreat. The Phoenicians would then go back to the shore and evaluate the offer. If the offer was not high enough, they would return to their ships and wait for a higher offer. This "silent trade" continued until both sides were satisfied.

sovereign, the warrior, the symbol of fertility and the creator of the world. Each town also had its own local gods.

Modern excavations have brought to light sacrificial sites, which are called tofets. Children or small animals were sacrificed at these sites. So far, tofets have been found only in colonies in North Africa at Carthage and Sousse (Hadrumetum), Motia (in Sicily) Sulcis and Tharsos (in Sardinia).

From the mollusc *Murex trunculus* a purple dye was extracted.

To make purple dye, the mollusc shell was cracked and the animal removed. The molluscs' bodies were then placed in large terracotta containers to rot in the sun. As the organic material decomposed, a purple dye was produced and used for dyeing cloth.

This upper portion of a stele found in Carthage bears an example of Phoenician writing.

This terracotta mask was found in Kurion, on the island of Cyprus.

On their ship, Phoenician merchants wait for people of the African coast to make an offering in gold in exchange for various goods. Displayed on the beach are vases, cloth, ostrich eggs and lapis lazuli.

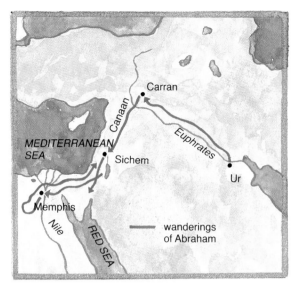

Abraham's journey from Ur to Canaan to Egypt and back to Canaan is marked in green.

The worship of the moon god was widespread throughout Babylon and was particularly important at Ur. This scene, reproduced from an Ur seal, dates from around 2000 B.C.

During the age of the patriarchs, one tribe rests at an oasis as another caravan arrives after crossing the desert.

ancient routes across the Sinai Peninsula

Part of the stele that celebrates the victory of Pharaoh Merneptah (around 1200 B.C.) is shown here. The word *Israel* carved in it is the earliest known mention of the name.

ISRAEL FROM ABRAHAM TO THE JUDGES

Abraham and the Origin of the Hebrew People

Abraham, who, according to the Bible, was the founder of the Hebrew people, lived around 1850 B.C. Abraham was a shepherd and a descendant of Shem, one of Noah's three sons. He was the "father of all the sons of Eber" of the family of Terah, and lived in the Sumerian town of Ur. Most likely, after the fall of the III Dynasty of Ur, Abraham and his relatives were forced to abandon their homeland. From there they travelled along the course of the Euphrates until they reached Haran. This migration through the Paddan Aram (or the Plain of Aram) is an important event in biblical history. The movement of

these people is recorded in historical documents of the peoples who lived in the region (Hittites and Hurrians).

The Arrival in Canaan and the Twelve Tribes

Guided by God's promise, Abraham made his way to the land of Canaan, with his wife Sarah and his nephew Lot. He led a semi-nomadic life, and stopped for a while in the southern areas close to the Negheb, which was sparsely populated and had no towns. The route of his wanderings is dotted with now-venerated sites, such as Sichem.

Abraham had two sons: Ishmael, who is considered the ancestor of the Arabs, and

Isaac. Ismael married in the land of Canaan, while Isaac chose his wife from among his people in Haran. Isaac had two sons, Esau and Jacob. Jacob, who was also called Israel, had twelve sons. These twelve sons are credited with heading the Twelve Tribes of Israel, the Israelites of the Bible.

The Exile in Egypt and the Exodus

When famine struck the land of Canaan, one of Jacob's sons, Joseph, led the Israelites to Egypt. There they settled in a region suitable for sheep farming and prospered. Soon they had attained much wealth and prestige, like Jacob before them. This prosperous period in

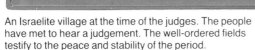
An Israelite village at the time of the judges. The people have met to hear a judgement. The well-ordered fields testify to the peace and stability of the period.

This map shows the paths that crossed the desert at the time of the Hebrew Exodus from Egypt. The triangles represent locations for Mount Sinai as proposed by various scholars.

A serpent mounted on a pole symbolizes the permanence of the Hebrew people in the desert. The Bible says that Moses protected his people against the threat of poisonous snakes by raising a bronze serpent, according to God's command.

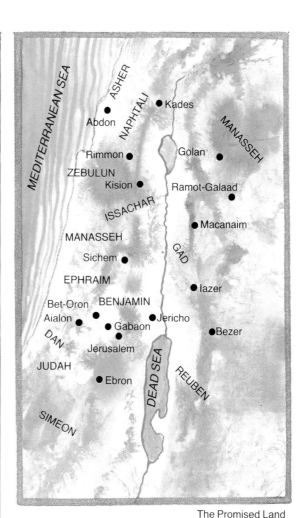

The Promised Land and the Twelve Tribes of Israel are shown on this map.

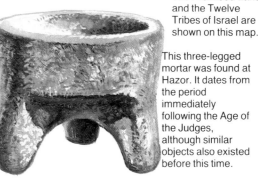

This three-legged mortar was found at Hazor. It dates from the period immediately following the Age of the Judges, although similar objects also existed before this time.

Egypt lasted only two hundred years, until the period of Egyptian revolt under the reigns of Ramses II (1298-1232 B.C.) and his successor Merneptah (1232-1224 B.C.). Under the new pharaoh, the Israelites lost their social positions and many were forced into slavery. The Israelites remained slaves until Moses led them from Egypt in 1200 B.C. This flight from Egypt, the Exodus, is the great event at the heart of Hebrew history and religion. It encompasses other important events such as the plagues of Egypt, the feast of The Passover, the miraculous escape, the presence of God upon Mount Sinai, the law of the Ten Commandments, the pilgrimage through the desert before reaching Canaan and the Promised Land.

The Return to Canaan: The Age of the Judges

Moses died before his people reached Canaan. However, under the leadership of his successor, Joshua, the Israelites crossed the River Jordan in the region of Jericho and settled in Canaan. This was a slow and difficult process that would last almost two hundred years. During this time, the Israelites were constantly at war with local peoples such as the Canaanites and the Philistines. Their culture had not prepared them for war. The division of the Hebrew people into twelve tribes made their armies weaker than those of their enemies.

In time, charismatic leaders, called judges, arose. A judge's influence was limited to one tribe and to control of local events. Eventually the tribes realized the need for a central government. They turned to Samuel, a judge who was respected by the majority of the people, and asked him to appoint a king. Around 1020 B.C., Samuel appointed Saul as the first king of Israel.

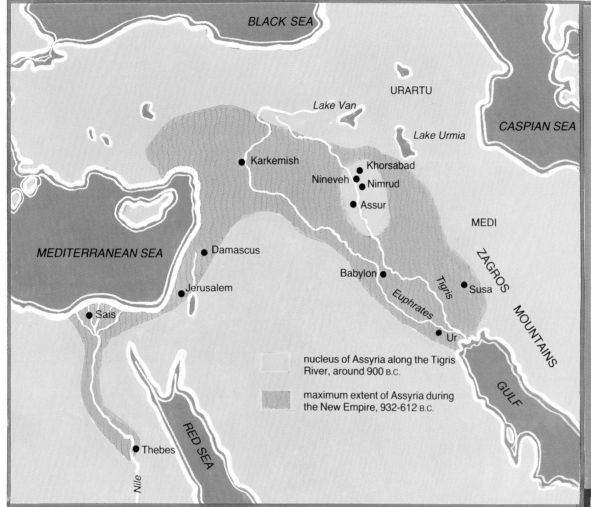

The Assyrian Empire stretched from the Mediterranean to the Gulf.

THE ASSYRIAN EMPIRE

The Assyrians were a group whose ancestors had been earlier Semitic migrants known as the Amorites. The immigration occurred throughout the region of Mesopotamia around 4000 years ago. The Assyrians settled the northern part of Mesopotamia, south of Lake Van and of the Armenian border, and west of the Zagros Mountains. To the south, their territory bordered the Babylonian kingdom.

The Ancient Empire

The history of the Assyrians begins at the end of the III Dynasty of Ur. This dynasty lost its power to the Amorite leaders of Assur, Babylon and Mari around 1950 B.C. The Ancient Assyrian Empire (1950-1365 B.C.) was a long period marked by a movement away from farming. During this time, trade became important and a large trade network developed, stretching primarily westward toward Anatolia. The Assyrians established colonies at important crossroads along the trade routes. This promising beginning for the Assyrians was interrupted by hostile invasions. At first they were defeated by Hammurabi, the king of Babylon. Later they were forced to surrender to the Hurrians.

The Middle Empire

The Middle Empire (1365-932 B.C.) was a period of Assyrian power, marked by the formation of a great empire. To the west, the Assyrians pushed as far as the Mediterranean, and to the southeast they conquered all of southern Mesopotamia. The Assyrians became increasingly rich, both economically and culturally. Economically, the fertility of the southern plain and the plentiful western forests were wealthy resources. Culturally, the empire advanced mainly through contact with the Babylonian and Sumerian cultures, both of which were more advanced. The Assyrian civilization came to be a great influence in the evolution of the ancient Middle East.

The New Empire

The New Empire (932-612 B.C.) marked the peak of Assyrian power. The army was strengthened by the addition of a cavalry which

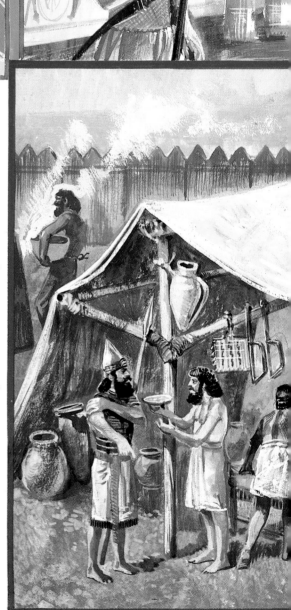

The Assyrian military camps were highly organized. Here, an officer's tent stands in the middle of the camp. Camels, seen in the background, were used for the first time during the reign of Ashurbanipal.

In the throne room of Nimrud, King Ashurnasirpal II (seated) meets with a dignitary. This Assyrian king reigned from 883-859 B.C.

admitted only members of the upper class and an infantry made up of people from all social groups. The monarchy continued to pursue the dream of a universal empire. (This dream was later to be passed on to the Persians and to Alexander the Great.)

In this period, the Assyrians earned their reputation as cruel and bloodthirsty warriors. They looted from conquered peoples to increase their own wealth and inspired terror in peoples near and far. The Assyrian army swarmed over the regions of Babylon, Urartu, Phoenicia, Syria, Palestine, Elam and Egypt.

The Assyrian king Tiglath-pileser III (745-727 B.C.) changed the shape of the whole eastern world. Under this ferocious and merciless king, Assyria became a tremendously powerful force. To control conquered populations, he would uproot the people of one country and transport them to another region. He also divided his empire into provinces that were governed by his own military officers. King Ashurbanipal (668-626 B.C.) concluded the campaigns against Egypt. After his death, Assyria began to decline. In 612 B.C. the Medes, with the Babylonians, invaded Assyria and destroyed Nineveh. After 609 B.C., the Assyrians vanished from history.

Ancient inscriptions, written for the Assyrian kings, describe their wars and victories:

From the *Prism* of King Sennacherib

"Hezekiah of Judah did not want to put himself beneath my yoke. I besieged forty-five of his forty-six towns and innumerable small villages nearby. I conquered them, building embankments, erecting siege towers, and pushing these close to the walls with assault troops . . . I looted the towns and deported, as prisoners, 200,150 people. . . . I imprisoned him (Hezekiah) in his residence in Jerusalem, like a bird in a cage. . . ."

From the *Annals* of Shalmaneser III (858-824 B.C.)

"In the eighteenth year of my reign, I crossed the Euphrates River for the sixteenth time. Azael, King of Damascus, trusting the strength of his army, gathered a great number of soldiers. . . . Fighting against him I inflicted a defeat: with my weapons, I overthrew the 16,000 soldiers of his army . . . I destroyed numberless towns, devastating them and burning them, and seizing great spoils. . ."

ASSYRIAN CIVILIZATION

Language and Literature

The language of the Assyrians, like that of the Babylonians, belonged to the Akkadian group. The only differences between the two languages were some symbols and rules of grammar. The two cultures had the same kind of writing; both used the cuneiform script.

Most Assyrian texts that still exist date back to the time of the New Empire and were preserved in the famous library of Ashurbanipal in Nineveh. Here this warrior sovereign collected Assyrian, Babylonian and Sumerian works. Many of these were copies from originals or copies of ancient tablets. These

laws themselves were unrefined and confusing. Society was organized on a military pattern, in the same way as the army.

Assyrians believed that the king's universal power was the will of the god Assur. This argument was used to justify wars and the cruel deeds that came with them. Gods, feasts, rituals and myths were the same as those of the Babylonians, and the similarities between the two religions were very great. The city of Assur was dedicated to the god, and the army's feats were also attributed to him. The sovereign was the god's visible representative and also served as the high priest in the

posture. Thus, it is difficult to distingui; them from other figures.

The bas-reliefs that decorated palace wal depicted scenes of royal life and mainly sho hunting, war or cultural scenes. They a among the most vivid expressions of Assyri; art. The most famous bas-reliefs are those the palace of Ashurbanipal in Nineveh. Al notable are the bronze plaques that formed tl doors of the palace of Shalmaneser III (85 824 B.C.) and those of the temple of Img' Enlil which depict the deeds of the kin Official seals also showed artistic qualit These seals depicted traditional images, su

The king Tukulti-Ninurta I worships a god represented by a flame on an altar.

In this bas-relief found in Nimrud, the tree of life stands between two winged spirits with eagles' heads. It may represent a spring festival, celebrating new life and fertility.

works included legends, historical accounts, prayers, legal documents, contracts and commemorative inscriptions. Especially important today are the *Annals*, which are records of the deeds of many sovereigns given in chronological order. From these writings it is possible to reconstruct Assyrian history from approximately 1000 B.C. These records even provide information on Assyrian war tactics and the loot seized in various battles.

Social and Religious Life

Assyrian law was the most merciless in all the Middle East. The guilty were often punished with beatings or mutilations, and the

religious rituals. Among the main gods worshipped were Ishtar (the goddess of love and war) and Adad (the god of natural phenomena).

Art

Assyrian art developed unique features during the Middle Empire and reached its height in the period of the New Empire. Architectural works included the ziggurat and the royal palaces. The most beautiful palace was that of King Sargon II in Dur Sharrukin. Sculptures shaped like lions and winged bulls with human heads were typical features of the royal palaces. The statues of the kings were highly stylized and did not have any obvious regal

as battles, winged spirits and sacred tree Despite Babylonian influence, Assyrian a had some unique features, especially in i celebration of the empire and the vivid scen taken from real life. These features are evide in wall-paintings or frescos, some of whic have survived to modern times.

Assyrian art is outstanding for the vigor and clarity with which it chronicles a lo world. The Assyrians were extraordinary sto; sculptors and metalworkers, and were al; skilled in carving ivory. Hundreds of ivoi objects were discovered during the excavatio of Nimrud. These pieces are of great interes both for their fine crafting and their themes.

An Assyrian king and his officers killing lions. The lions are released into a previously prepared clearing. From the many hunting scenes in Assyrian art, it is clear that hunting was a favourite royal pastime.

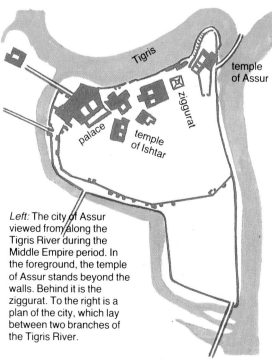

Left: The city of Assur viewed from along the Tigris River during the Middle Empire period. In the foreground, the temple of Assur stands beyond the walls. Behind it is the ziggurat. To the right is a plan of the city, which lay between two branches of the Tigris River.

THE HURRIANS OF URARTU

The name *Urartu*, referring to what is now Armenia, is first found in Assyrian inscriptions of the thirteenth century B.C. This evidence exists in an account of King Shalmaneser I's recovery of control over seven rebel states in the Urartu region. The Assyrians were very skilled soldiers. But even so, they had problems controlling provinces that were as hard to reach as mountainous Urartu.

In the ninth century, this region was inhabited by Hurrian tribes united under King Aramu. Aramu was defeated by Shalmaneser III. Some scholars believe that the name *Armenia* given later to this area was derived from King Aramu's name.

The Urartean Kings

King Sarduri I moved the capital to Van. King Menua I (810-785 B.C.) expanded his dominion to the west to gain an outlet onto the Mediterranean coast. He built temples, palaces and towns and encouraged the construction of irrigation systems all over the region. King Argishti I (785-760 B.C.) extended his kingdom even farther and founded the towns of Erebum and Argishtihinili.

Life in the kingdom of Urartu was affected by the Assyrian presence, which prevented expansion to the west. The Assyrians also constantly invaded the southern part of the kingdom near lakes Urmia and Van. Urartean attempts to expand to the east were stopped by the Medes, Indo-Europeans who had settled there.

In 743 and 735 B.C., Urartu was defeated by the Assyrian king Tiglath-pileser II. This marked the beginning of its decline. The kingdom was again sacked in 714 B.C. by Sargon II. Eventually, during the reign of King Sarduri III (645-625 B.C.), the kingdom of Urartu became a client state of Assyria. It remained in Assyria's possession until the fall of Nineveh (612 B.C.) to the Medes and Scythians. King Rusa III (605-590 B.C.) was the last to leave inscriptions about the major events of his reign. With his death, the kingdom of Urartu collapsed.

Commerce and Agriculture

Hurrian expansion had both military and economic reasons behind it. These people primarily traded iron, silver and gold objects made from metals from the mines of the Taurus region in Cilicia. They also controlled the goods coming from Phoenicia and Syria Minor and from the main east-west trade routes. The Hurrians were also skilled metalworkers, and they traded metal goods over long distances. They increased the effectiveness of their region through the construction of major irrigation systems, and so were able to farm previously uncultivated lands.

Architecture and Art

Most of the identified architectural remains are citadels or fortified towns with large brick walls built on a stone base. Excavations by archaeologists show that a building's ground floor was used as a storage space, while the upper level was used as a home.

Due to the geographical location and fea-

a	b	g	d	e	z	ē	ə	t'	ž
i	l	x	c	k	h	j	ł	č	m

The Language

The Hurrians spoke an Indo-European language. In their writing, they used cuneiform characters, as did Assyrians and Babylonians. However, the new populations which developed in Armenia after the breakup of the empire abandoned this language and writing. They memorized the events of their history and resorted to the Persian, Aramaic and Greek languages. This continued until the fifth century A.D. when Saint Mesrop Mashtolz invented the Armenian alphabet. The Armenian language attained great importance among the Indo-European languages. The most ancient Armenian literature is almost entirely made up of translations of Greek works.

tures of the kingdom, the art of Urartu was heavily influenced by that of the Assyrians, and partially by the Medes. Bronze objects are almost the only evidence of this art. Large cauldrons are among the most typical objects.

From Urartu to Armenia

After the fall of the Hurrian kingdom, the region was invaded by various tribes coming from the north, such as the Scythians and the Cimmerians. These peoples used the tight network of trade routes when invading the region. A Babylonian inscription from the reign of Darius in 520 B.C. still calls the region Urartu; a parallel Persian inscription calls it Armenia. In 500 B.C., the Greek geographer Hecataeus spoke of the "Armenian" people. The terms *Armenia* and *Armenians* were probably originally used by some Iranian tribes, and only later by Romans and Greeks.

This bronze sphinx was part of a throne found in Toprakkale (800-700 B.C.).

MEDITERRANEAN SEA

This drawing shows a storage room with jars for wine and other products on the ground floor of an Urartean house in Karmir Blur.

A cauldron handle shaped like a bull's head from Toprakkale.

BLACK SEA

Front view of the temple of Musasir.

territory of Urartu

This bronze lion was found at Kayalidere.

trade route towards Asia Minor

ARMENIA MINOR

Lake Sevan

Armavir

Erebun

Kermir Blur

ARMENIA MAJOR

Kayalidere

Lake Van

Toprakkale

Tushpa (Van)

Lake Urmia

CASPIAN SEA

trade route towards Italy

Tigris

Euphrates

Musasir

Nineveh

SYRIA

This bronze cauldron comes from Gordium and dates from the eighth century B.C.

CYPRUS

A partial view of the castle walls at Toprakkale.

MEDI

trade route towards the Far East

Bronze helmets date from the Argishti period between 800 and 700 B.C.

Ararat is an extinct volcano which dominates the Armenian plateau. This plateau was the site on which the kingdom of Urartu developed.

GULF

A handle from a bronze cauldron in the shape of a siren's head. The cauldron, dating from around 700 B.C., was found in Gordium.

RED SEA

ANATOLIA IN THE FIRST MILLENNIUM B.C.

By about 1000 B.C., the Anatolia peninsula (modern Turkey) was populated by massive migrations of people who settled, in successive waves, over a period of several centuries. These peoples were of Indo-European origin. Around 1200 B.C., they moved into Anatolia from Europe as well as from the sea (the Sea People). Others came from the Eurasian steppes in the following centuries.

With each invasion, towns were destroyed and the countryside devastated. Some states would fall while others took advantage of the situation. For example, the Phrygians contributed to the collapse of the Hittite Empire. Cimmerians too gained from the downfall of other states.

The Rise of the Kingdom of the Phrygians

The Phrygia region included the western part of the Anatolian plateau. Around 1200 B.C., this region was invaded by peoples who probably came from Thrace and Macedonia. In the beginning, this area was divided into small kingdoms. These later joined together and formed a powerful, centrally governed kingdom whose capital was Gordium. This state reached the height of its power under King Midas, who fought against the Assyrian king Sargon II and established relationships with Greece. Between 900 and 600 B.C., the Aegean Sea was controlled by the Phrygians. They maintained their independence until they were conquered by the Cimmerians in 695 B.C. The Cimmerians in turn fell to the Lydians in 585 B.C. Finally, in 546 B.C., the Persian army conquered the whole territory.

The Culture of the Phrygians

Phrygian art has come to light in excavations in the towns of Gordium, Eskisehir, Ancira, Alaca, Kültepe and Bogazköy. Typical architecture includes tombs and temples decorated with lions and geometrical patterns. Burial mounds containing precious objects were found in Gordium. The use of bronze and ivory was a typical feature of Phrygian art.

The Phrygians spoke an Indo-European language that is known through stone carvings and inscriptions. The oldest inscriptions were found near Gordium and date back to 600 B.C. A more recent form of Phrygian language, called Neo-Phrygian, developed around 300 B.C. Examples were found on inscriptions

unearthed south of Gordium. The Phrygian alphabet was very similar to that of ancient Greek.

The Kingdom of Lydia

Lydia included the western and southern parts of Anatolia. It had a long history and was highly civilized. It was also an important trade centre because of the many natural harbours on its coast facing the Aegean Sea. The Lydians were probably of Indo-European origin, but the date of their arrival in the region is uncertain. They are first mentioned in accounts from the seventh century B.C.

The Heraclidae dynasty ruled Lydia for 505 years. The last king of the Heraclidae dynasty was Candaules, who was killed in 685 B.C. by a rival named Gyges. Gyges then founded the Mermnads dynasty. The last king of this dynasty was Croesus (560-546 B.C.), under whose guidance Lydia became a true empire. It stretched over territories on both sides of the Halys River and included the Greek towns of the Ionia region. Croesus reigned until 546 B.C. when King Cyrus of Persia conquered Lydia.

The Lydians were wealthy and sophisticated. They were among the first people to use money, in the seventh century B.C. Their art followed Greek and eastern models, with favourite subjects being lions and sphinxes. Particularly interesting are the hundreds of huge burial mounds.

The Lycians

The southeastern extremity of Asia Minor is covered by a plateau and by mountain chains. Before the Greeks arrived, this area was inhabited by the Lycians. According to the Greek historian Herodotus, the Lycians were a pirate people from the island of Crete. In the sixth century B.C., the region became part of the Persian Empire.

The Lycian language was an Indo-European language that has not yet been completely decoded. Examples of it are provided by inscriptions dating from between 500 and 300 B.C. The only examples of Lycian art are grave monuments that were found in the region's main towns.

On the large map, the kingdoms of Anatolia are shown. The small map traces migrations of Indo-European peoples.

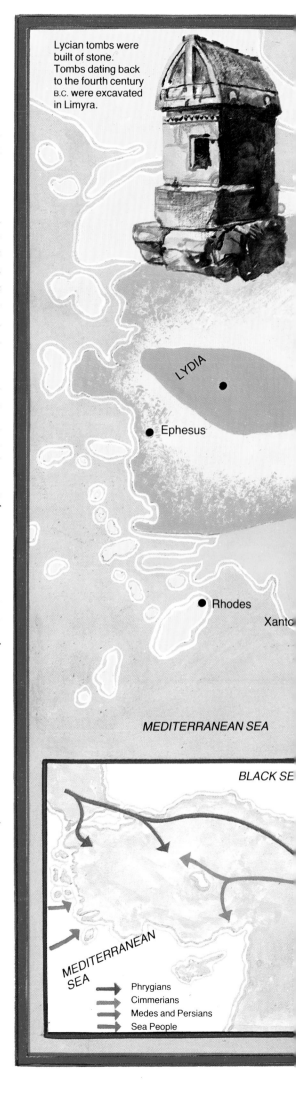

Lycian tombs were built of stone. Tombs dating back to the fourth century B.C. were excavated in Limyra.

LYDIA

Ephesus

Rhodes

Xanto

MEDITERRANEAN SEA

BLACK SE

MEDITERRANEAN SEA

Phrygians
Cimmerians
Medes and Persians
Sea People

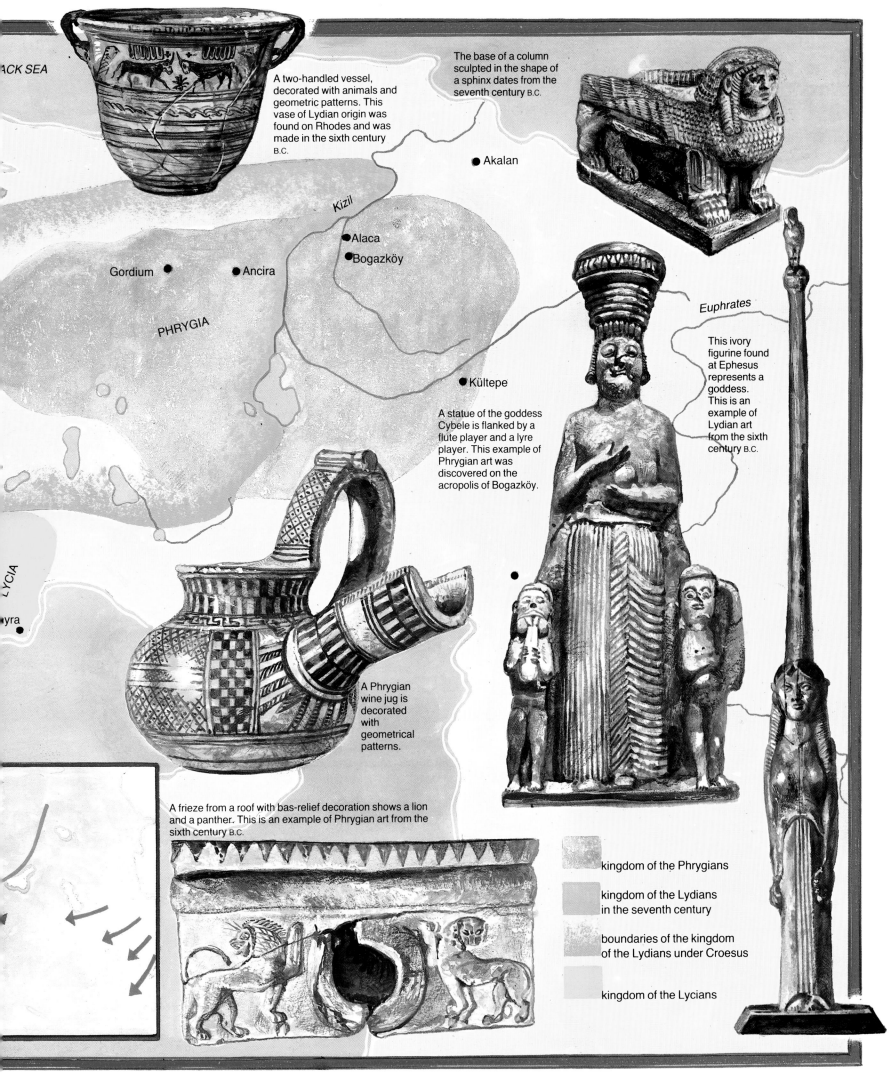

ACK SEA

A two-handled vessel, decorated with animals and geometric patterns. This vase of Lydian origin was found on Rhodes and was made in the sixth century B.C.

The base of a column sculpted in the shape of a sphinx dates from the seventh century B.C.

● Akalan

Kizil

● Alaca
● Bogazköy

Gordium ●   ● Ancira

PHRYGIA

● Kültepe

Euphrates

A statue of the goddess Cybele is flanked by a flute player and a lyre player. This example of Phrygian art was discovered on the acropolis of Bogazköy.

This ivory figurine found at Ephesus represents a goddess. This is an example of Lydian art from the sixth century B.C.

LYCIA

●yra

A Phrygian wine jug is decorated with geometrical patterns.

A frieze from a roof with bas-relief decoration shows a lion and a panther. This is an example of Phrygian art from the sixth century B.C.

kingdom of the Phrygians

kingdom of the Lydians in the seventh century

boundaries of the kingdom of the Lydians under Croesus

kingdom of the Lycians

The Israelites enter the town of Jerusalem after conquering it.

The temple built by King Solomon in Jerusalem became the sacred centre of the monotheistic (one-god) religion of the Israelites.

ISRAEL— FROM THE KINGS TO EXILE

When the Israelites occupied Canaan, they preferred to settle in sparsely populated hilly areas. They avoided the villages and small towns, which were then in the hands of the Canaanites, as well as the fortified towns, often ruled by Philistine tribes. The region's coastal areas were divided among Canaanites and Philistines.

Religion was the great unifying force among the Twelve Tribes of Israel. Their religion, Judaism, however, involved an element of weakness. The worship of a single god and the absence of representations of that god, meant that the religion was constantly in danger of being absorbed by local polytheistic religions.

The Kings

The king of Israel was unlike any other king in the ancient world. His legislative power was very limited. For one thing, he was regarded as the enforcer of divine laws rather than a lawmaker. The first king, appointed by Samuel, was Saul, a member of the tribe of Benjamin. Backed by his people, Saul undertook a series of victorious battles against the Philistines and others who lived in Canaan. Saul died on the battlefield with his son, Jonathan.

David, of the tribe of Judah, succeeded Saul and ruled from 1010 to 970 B.C. David was the greatest king of Israel. He brilliantly ended the war against the Philistines, expanded the kingdom's boundaries both to the north and to the south, and gave the twelve tribes a kingdom so vast that it remained unequalled in Jewish history. David, a shrewd politician, sought to unify the tribes. For his capital, he chose a town which was not yet inhabited by any tribe and occupied it himself. The town, called Jebus, was later renamed Jerusalem. In Jerusalem, David chose the sites where the Temple, the royal palace, and all the government buildings were to be built. The construction of the new Jerusalem was completed by David's son and successor, Solomon, who ruled from 970 to 931 B.C. Solomon divided Israel into provinces, or military districts, strengthened the border towns with fortresses, and greatly improved sea trade.

The Division of the Kingdom

On Solomon's death, the tribes of the northern areas broke away from the dynasty of David and from Jerusalem. Thus the country was divided into two kingdoms: Israel to the north, and Judah to the south. The first king of the northern kingdom was Jeroboam (931-910 B.C.). The southern kingdom was ruled by Solomon's son Rehoboam (931-913 B.C.).

The northern kingdom was much more wealthy and powerful than the southern king-

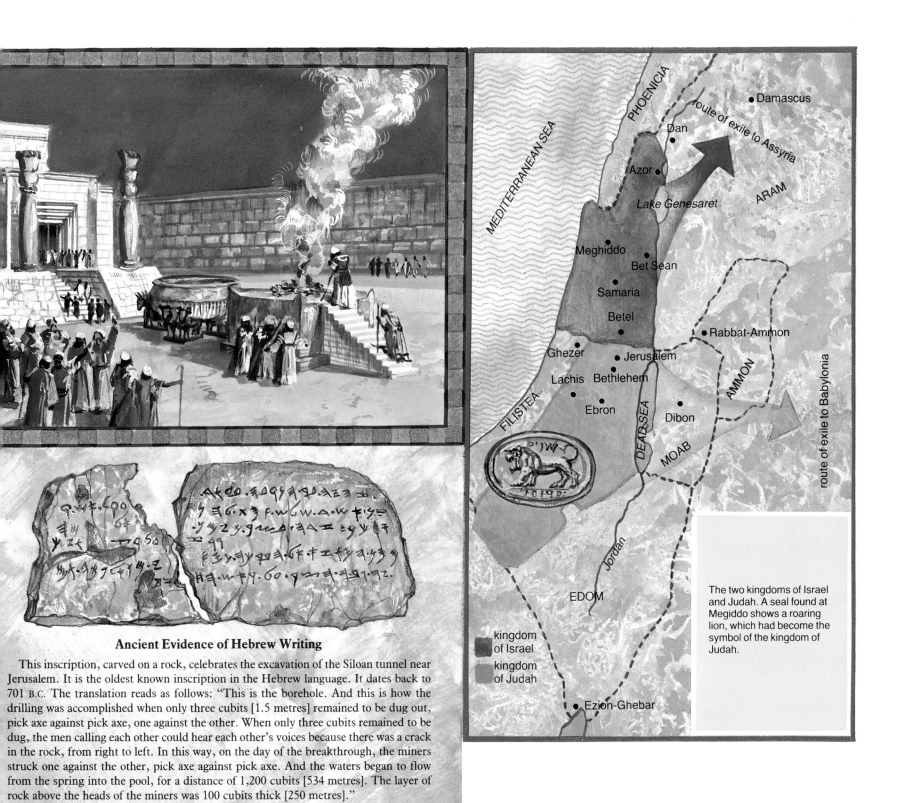

Ancient Evidence of Hebrew Writing

This inscription, carved on a rock, celebrates the excavation of the Siloan tunnel near Jerusalem. It is the oldest known inscription in the Hebrew language. It dates back to 701 B.C. The translation reads as follows: "This is the borehole. And this is how the drilling was accomplished when only three cubits [1.5 metres] remained to be dug out, pick axe against pick axe, one against the other. When only three cubits remained to be dug, the men calling each other could hear each other's voices because there was a crack in the rock, from right to left. In this way, on the day of the breakthrough, the miners struck one against the other, pick axe against pick axe. And the waters began to flow from the spring into the pool, for a distance of 1,200 cubits [534 metres]. The layer of rock above the heads of the miners was 100 cubits thick [250 metres]."

The two kingdoms of Israel and Judah. A seal found at Megiddo shows a roaring lion, which had become the symbol of the kingdom of Judah.

om, but it was troubled by internal problems. One problem was the struggle for royal power, with several families trying to get control. Different royal families were continually succeeding each other in the northern kingdom. Another problem troubling the kingdom was a series of fierce religious disputes between the followers of the traditional religion and those who wanted to include within it worship of local Canaanite deities.

The most important kings of the north were: Ahab (874-853 B.C.), who married the Canaanite woman Jezebel and opposed the prophet Elijah; Joram (852-841 B.C.) and Jehu (841-814 B.C.), who led a war against King Mesha of Moab; Menahem (743-738 B.C.) and Pekah (737-732 B.C.), who headed the clashes with the Assyrian king Tiglathpileser III and were defeated; and finally, Hosea (732-724 B.C.). Under Hosea's rule, Samaria, the capital, was attacked by King Shalmaneser V. Eventually, the northern kingdom was defeated and its people were deported by Sargon II in 721 B.C.

The End of Judah

The history of the kingdom of Judah was more peaceful. Its most important kings were: Hezekiah (716-687 B.C.), who lost some towns to Sargon II and endured the siege of Jerusalem; Manasseh (687-642 B.C.), who had to pay tribute to the Assyrian kings Esarhaddon and Ashurbanipal; and Josiah (640-609 B.C.), who began a programme of religious reform and died in battle against the Egyptian pharaoh Neco II. In this period, the Babylonian Empire regained its strength as the Assyrian dominance drew towards its end. The Babylonian king Nebuchadrezzar crushed the kingdom of Judah in 604 B.C. Jerusalem was sacked and the king and most of the people deported to Babylonia.

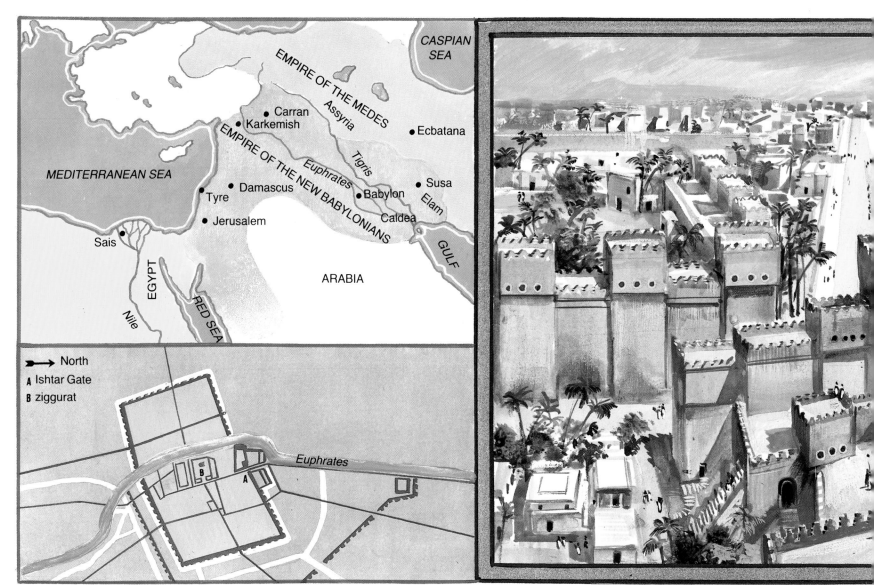

Top: A map of the New Babylonian Empire. Below it is a plan of the city of Babylon as it developed along the Euphrates River between 700 and 500 B.C.

THE NEW BABYLONIANS

In spite of Assyria's constant victories and expansion, the Assyrian Empire's frontiers on three sides were constantly exposed to attacks from outsiders. The ceaseless wars brought wealth to the empire but exhausted the population. The king Ashurbanipal repulsed many attacks on the empire, including those on the region of Elam which formed its southern part. After the king's death in 631 B.C., however, the empire collapsed and never regained its strength. In 626 B.C., the Chaldaean general Nabopolassar seized Babylon and proclaimed its independence from the Assyrian Empire. He founded the XI Chaldaean dynasty, also called the New Babylonian dynasty. In 616 B.C., he declared war on Assyria and made an alliance with the Medes. The Egyptian pharaoh Psammetichus joined the war on the side of Assyria, but the city of Nineveh fell before his arrival in 612 B.C.

The Assyrian and Egyptian armies clashed with the armies of the Medes and of Nabopolassar at Carchemish in 605 B.C. This was the last great battle fought by the Assyrians. In it, the young general of Nabopolassar, Nebuchadrezzar, proved his great courage. After the battle, the Egyptians went back home, while the New Babylonians and Medes, led by King Cyaxares, renewed their alliance and agreed to destroy completely the Assyrian kingdom.

Nebuchadrezzar's Kingdom

Under Nabopolassar's successor, Nebuchadrezzar (605-562 B.C.), the New Babylonian kingdom reached its greatest splendour. The king enlarged the territory that he had inherited, conquering Syria, the city of Tyre and all of Phoenicia. He also conquered the kingdom of Judah, in Palestine, destroying Jerusalem

Builder Kings

The first New Babylonian kings were very active builders. They put all of their energy into the reconstruction of the capital, Babylon. They erected a double wall around the city, which was located on the River Euphrates. Inside the defensive walls were splendid living quarters and terraces. Babylon is famous for the beautiful hanging gardens created on some of the terraces. The ziggurat, a monument later called the Tower of Babel, and its temple to the god Marduk, dominated the entire city.

Nebuchadrezzar's works were celebrated in an inscription as follows: "I have completed the construction of Babylon, the sublime city / the city of his majesty (Marduk) / and its great walls. / By its entrance doors I have put giant bulls, / a thing that no one had ever done before. / My father surrounded the city with two walls made of tar and fired bricks, / I erected a third strong wall, made of tar and fired bricks / and joined it to the walls of my father."

and its Temple in 587 B.C. From the Assyrians Nebuchadrezzar learned the practice of exiling the defeated aristocrats and merchants from their homeland.

Nabonidus: The Last Gleam

The reign of Nebuchadrezzar was followed

A view of Babylon shows the Ishtar Gate and an avenue called the Processional Street. In the upper right corner, the hanging gardens and the ziggurat with the Temple of Marduk are shown.

Examples of Babylonian art. Panels of coloured brick depict two symbolic animals: the lion of the Processional Street and the dragon of the Ishtar Gate.

An illustration of the ziggurat of Babylon. This building was called "the house of the foundations of heaven and earth". It was over 90 metres high and was topped with a small temple. This temple was sacred to Marduk, the resident god of the city.

by a brief period of decline that ended in the empire's final collapse. The last New Babylonian king was Nabonidus (556-539 B.C.). He vainly resisted the increasing power of the Persians and retreated for a time to the oasis of Teiman on the Arabian border. This retreat was the origin of several legends. One legend held that the king made this retreat because of a personal religious experience. It seems more likely that he tried to organize Arab tribes to defend the New Babylonian Empire. Nabonidus had made religious reforms, resulting in disagreement with the priests. The priests therefore rejoiced in his eventual defeat when the Persian king Cyrus invaded New Babylonia in 539 B.C. Entering the city of Babylon without striking a blow, Cyrus ended the short triumph of the New Babylonian kingdom.

Culture and Society

The culture and art of the Babylonians always commanded great prestige in ancient Mesopotamia. The Babylonians maintained this position during most of the centuries of the Persian Empire, and their influence was evident in writing, language, philosophy and religion. Their literature was extremely rich, and many of their documents still exist. Babylonian society was organized in a pyramidal structure. At the top was the king, who was the supreme military, religious and political leader. The economy of the kingdom was based on agriculture, livestock-raising and artisan activities that were sometimes highly specialized. Commerce and trade, both by river and by land, was highly developed.

THE PERSIANS

The Persians and the Achaemenid Dynasty

The name *Persians* is mentioned for the first time in Assyrian documents of the ninth century B.C. At that time, nomadic tribes of Medes and Persians had settled on the Iranian plateau (territory that includes parts of modern Iran and Afghanistan), where they lived as shepherds and farmers. By the seventh century B.C., the Medes had established the kingdom of Media on the northern end of the plateau and conquered the Persians, who had settled to the south. From there, the Medes moved west and conquered Susa and the lands of Elam. Towards the end of the seventh century B.C., the Medes fought against the Assyrians, in alliance with the Babylonians. Nineveh, Assyria's capital, fell in 612 B.C. Soon afterwards all of Assyria was conquered.

About 550 B.C., the Persians, led by Cyrus the Great, overthrew the Medes. With the Median lands in their possession, the Persians established a very powerful empire. Cyrus, who was a member of the Achaemenid dynasty, became its first ruler. This is why the empire came to be called the Achaemenid Empire. Ecbatana, the capital of Media, became the summer residence of the court of the Achaemenids. The ancient city of Pasargadae became their sacred city and Cyrus ordered that his tomb be erected there.

Under Cyrus the Great, Anatolia also became a Persian province. Later, the regions of Sogdiana and Bactria were added to the empire. In 539 B.C., the New Babylonian kingdom was defeated, and still later the people of Syria, Phoenicia and Palestine came under Persian rule.

Persia's Empire Expands

Cyrus's son, Cambyses II, became his successor. Cambyses expanded the empire's territory to include Egypt and Cyrenaica, but he also had to cope with numerous rebellions.

Darius I, who became king in 522 B.C., eventually conquered the rebellious provinces and put an end to the turmoil. First, he enlarged the kingdom's eastern borders as far as the upper reaches of the Indus River. Then he turned west and conquered Thrace and Macedonia. He also conducted an unsuccessful campaign against the Scythians in the region of the lower reaches of the Danube. Meanwhile, the Persians had their eyes on Greece. Darius declared war against Athens, but the hostilities were concluded at the Battle of Marathon with the victory of the Athenians in 490 B.C. Darius died in 486 B.C.

In 486 B.C., Xerxes I succeeded his father Darius. He soon re-established Persian power and prestige in the western provinces. He regained control of Thrace and Macedonia and also penetrated into Boeotia and Thessaly. Leonidas, king of Sparta, tried to stop Xerxes at Thermopylae, north of Athens, but was defeated in battle. Athens was conquered in 480 B.C. However, shortly after, in the Battle of Salamis, the Greek fleet ambushed the Persian navy, destroying about half of the fleet. At this point, Xerxes' drive to control Greece had lost momentum. He returned home to Persia, leaving his general, Mardonius, in command. A final battle took place at Plataea in 479 B.C. There the Greeks again defeated the Persian army and put an end to the invasion.

Xerxes' death in 465 B.C. signalled a decline for the Achaemenid Empire. Although the empire continued to exist, it was plagued by constant struggles, military clashes and internal problems. Finally, in 331 B.C., Alexander the Great led the Macedonians to a victory over the Persian army in the Battle of Arbela. With this defeat, the Achaemenid Empire came to an end.

Right: The map shows the Achaemenid Empire at its peak under Darius (522-486 B.C.). *Top and bottom of page:* Part of the frieze which decorated the staircase of the famous palace of Persepolis, the capital of the empire founded by Darius I around 516 B.C. and enlarged by his son Xerxes. The frieze shows a procession of delegates from the twenty-eight conquered nations bringing gifts to the king.

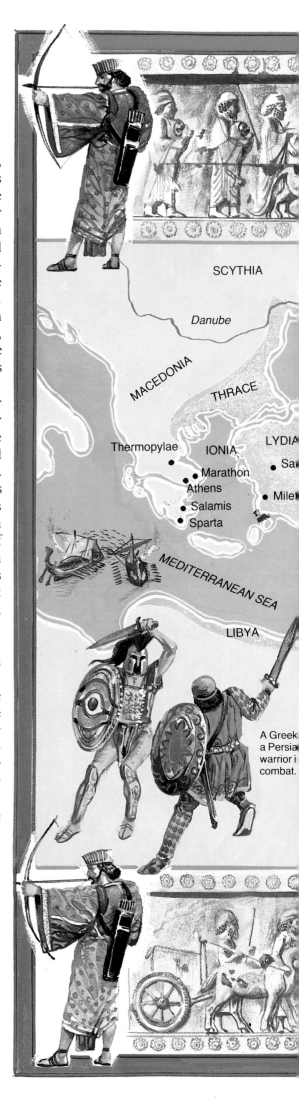

SCYTHIA

Danube

MACEDONIA

THRACE

Thermopylae

IONIA

LYDIA

Marathon

Sa

Athens

Mile

Salamis

Sparta

MEDITERRANEAN SEA

LIBYA

A Greek
a Persia
warrior i
combat.

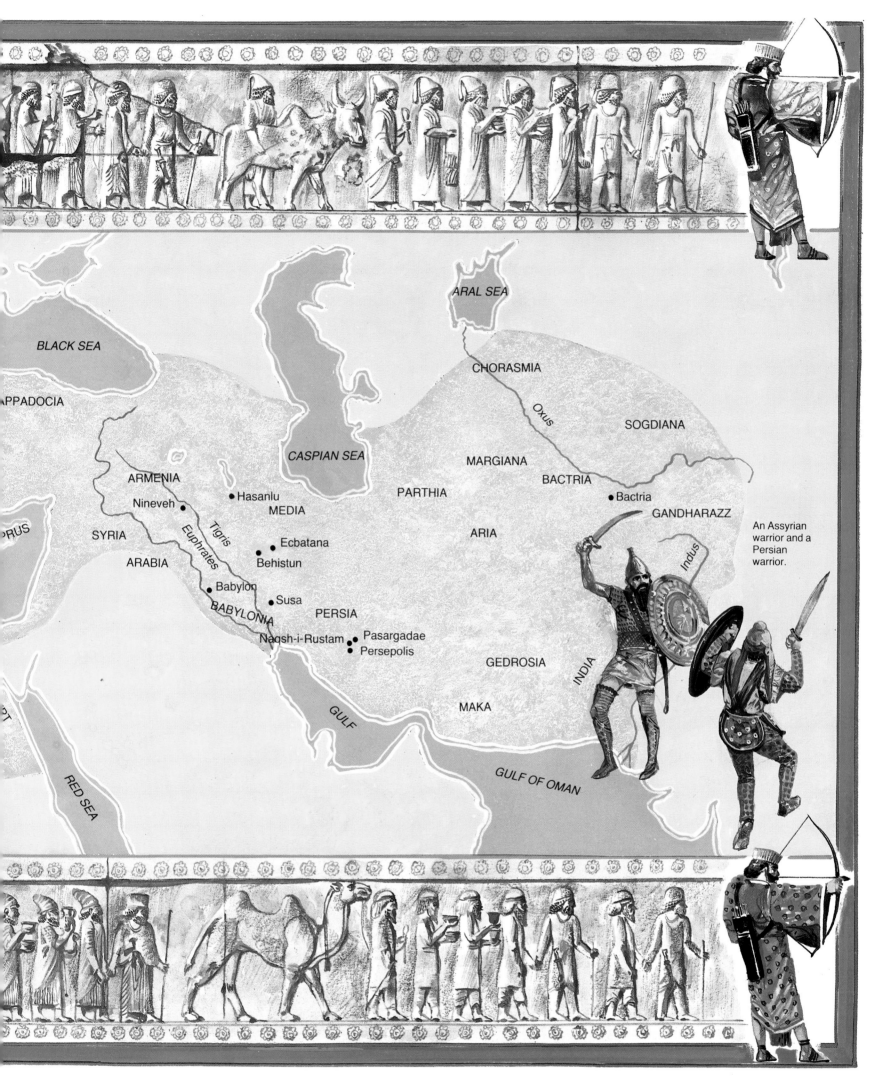

ARAL SEA

BLACK SEA

CHORASMIA

Oxus

SOGDIANA

MARGIANA

CASPIAN SEA

BACTRIA

APPADOCIA

ARMENIA

PARTHIA

• Bactria

Nineveh •

• Hasanlu

MEDIA

GANDHARAZZ

RUS

Tigris

Euphrates

ARIA

SYRIA

• Ecbatana

Indus

ARABIA

• Behistun

An Assyrian
warrior and a
Persian
warrior.

• Babylon

BABYLONIA

• Susa

PERSIA

Naqsh-i-Rustam
• • Pasargadae
• Persepolis

INDIA

RED SEA

GULF

GEDROSIA

MAKA

GULF OF OMAN

45

THE ACHAEMENID EMPIRE

The Achaemenid Empire began with Cyrus the Great. Under his rule, Persian imperialism was characterized by mercy and fairness towards conquered peoples. Such qualities were unusual to say the least, in a region traditionally used to memories of fierce Assyrian rule. Conquered princes were not tortured or killed and were sometimes given positions within the empire's administration. The king's authority was absolute, but he was helped by an assembly of nobles. People of various nationalities were employed in the imperial administration. Only the army was composed mainly of Medes and Persians.

Taxes were collected fairly, although Medes and Persians were granted a certain degree of privilege in their payments. The various con-

Improved roads allowed for rapid communication throughout the empire. An example of this is the famous Royal Road which connected Susa, in the heart of the empire, to Sardis, in Lydia, covering a distance of over 2,400 kilometres. This road was safe from attacks by bandits, and provided with "service areas" where horses could be replaced, and travellers could eat and rest.

The First Great Empire

Under the kings Cyrus the Great and Darius I, the Persians conquered many of the ancient Near East and Middle East civilizations, absorbing them into their empire. For the first time in history, Mesopotamia, Syria, Egypt, Asia Minor, numerous Greek towns and par

Left, above: A bas-relief from the sixth century B.C. shows a likeness of Darius I. It was found in Behistun.

The illustration shows a relay station, for changing horses, on the Royal Road. The map (*bottom left*) shows the route of the Royal Road from Sardis near the Mediterranean Sea, to Susa, one of the four capitals of the Achaemenid Empire.

The King of Kings

Darius I ordered that two tablets, a gold one and a silver one, be placed within the foundations of the palace of Persepolis in remembrance of its construction. The text, written in ancient Persian, in Babylonian and in Elamite, reads as follows: "This is the kingdom which I own, stretching from the country of the Saka people, who live on this side of the Sogdiana, to the country of Kush, from India to Sardis. Here is what Ahura Mazda has bestowed on me, he who is the foremost of all the gods. May Ahura Mazda protect me and my family." Ahura Mazda was the god of the Persian religion, Zoroastrianism.

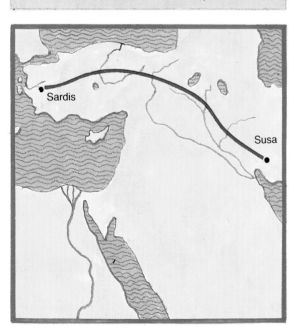

quered populations were allowed to retain their religions, laws, customs, and sometimes even their leaders, provided they recognized the authority of the king. The empire was divided into provinces, called satrapies. Each satrapy was ruled by a "protector of the kingdom". This protector administered justice, maintained order and collected taxes. He was also the commander of the local militia, although larger armies were led by a general responsible to the king.

Within the empire, major efforts were made to carry out public works. These included drainage, irrigation systems and road construction. The Persians were the first to use camels as transport animals. They established commercial relationships with peoples in remote areas, significantly increasing their trade.

The Persian Language

Persian is an Indo-European language, closely related to the Sanskrit language. In its ancient form, it was written with cuneiform characters, as shown by rock inscriptions made during the period between the reigns of Darius and Artaxerxes III (from 600-300 B.C.). It was based on an Iranian dialect used by the court.

Another form of Persian language is Avestan. This was a more refined language used in sacred texts (called *Avesta*) which contained the philosophy of Zoroaster. The language used between 250 B.C. and A.D. 650 is called Middle Persian or Pahlavi. This is a complex language which was used to write commentaries on the *Avesta*. The common language spoken throughout the Persian empire from Egypt to India was Aramaic, a language of the Semitic group.

Darius I receives envoys from Persian-ruled territories.

of India were united under one king. The Persians did not impose their civilization on the peoples of their empire. Among the lands they conquered were those with ancient civilizations, more advanced than Persia's own civilization. Cyrus and Darius granted wide freedom to these territories and promoted the preservation of their different cultures. This policy resulted in pronounced cultural differences between the Persians and the conquered peoples which eventually led to the empire's fall.

The Persians' tolerant policy had great historical importance. The principles by which the Persians ruled their empire of many cultures remained alive even after the empire had fallen. Alexander the Great adopted them, and from the Hellenistic world, they were eventually transmitted to modern Europe.

THE PERSIAN GOVERNMENT

KING OF KINGS
The supreme ruler or emperor

COUNCIL OF THE EMPEROR
Formed by nobles representing all the peoples of the empire

SATRAPS
Usually veteran generals; one at the head of each large province, or satrapy; heads of the civilian administration and of local militia

GENERALS
Commanders of the royal troops; chosen from Median and Persian soldiers; stationed at the various satrapies

PEOPLES OF THE EMPIRE
Each people was ruled by its own laws, traditions and customs and led by its own rulers

PERSIAN RELIGION AND ART

Ahura Mazda, the most important Persian deity, is depicted with the winged wheel, a symbol of the sky.

This building was found near the royal tombs of Naqsh-i-Rustam.

This altar, discovered in Naqsh-i-Rustam, dates back to the third century B.C.

The magi were priests of the ancient Persian religion. This drawing is based on an image on a gold plate found near the Oxus River. The plate dates from between 700 and 500 B.C.

The Religion of Zoroaster

Persian religion was extremely rich. According to tradition, it was inspired by the teachings of Zoroaster, a philosopher-mystic who lived around 600 B.C. Zoroaster called for changes and improvements in the ancient Persian religion. He acquired a small group of followers. His followers had to abandon the ancient tradition of sacrificing a bull to the gods. Knowledge of his teachings comes through the sacred texts, called *Avesta*, which survive to this day.

The core of Zoroaster's doctrine and preaching is morality, people's behaviour and actions. He was obsessed by the idea that the wicked would be punished, and the virtuous would be rewarded. He taught that each person was free to choose a path in life, and that in choosing the way of the god Ahura Mazda, one was making the right choice. At the end of life, each human being would be judged according to the choices he or she had made. Those who had made the right choices would be welcomed into paradise. Sinners would dwell in the house of evil forever.

Ahura Mazda was the just and supreme god who constantly fought against evil. He would triumph at the end of time. In addition to Ahura Mazda, a god of light always depicted emerging from a winged sun, there were two other gods: Mithras and Anahit. As Ahura Mazda's representative, the Persian king's responsibility was to see that justice triumphed at all times. He was also to allow all people to live according to their own laws. These religious concepts might have influenced Cyrus's decision to allow the Jewish people, exiled in Babylonia, to return to their homeland.

Persian Art

Early Persian art bore reminders of the art of the steppe tribes. Examples were discovered during archaeological excavations in numerous necropolises (cemeteries). The necropolis of Siyalk is made up of tombs of people from all social classes. Excavations in this necropolis revealed bangles, earrings and ceramics decorated with geometrical patterns, and animal and human figures. The tombs of Khurvin show different artistic tendencies, while excavations in Hasanlu revealed art objects with fantastic shapes.

The most outstanding art forms produced by these early Persian peoples were highly original bronze and iron objects from Luristan during the seventh century B.C. Through these materials, the artists expressed an extraordinarily elaborate mythology. During the two centuries of the Achaemenid dynasty, Persian art centred on the monarch. All art was meant to celebrate and praise the monarchy and to enhance the feeling that all the people were part of one political entity. The artists were influenced by artistic styles from the various lands of the empire, especially by Mesopotamian art.

Since the Persians were great builders of towns, courts and temples, knowledge of their art has been known mainly through the ruins of the various capitals: Ecbatana, Pasargadae, Susa and Persepolis. In each capital, the central and most important monument was the royal palace, which was used as a residence, a treasury, and a site for receptions and public audiences. At the centre of the palace was the audience chamber, its ceiling supported by several rows of columns. The palace was decorated with winged bulls, figures of spirits, monumental staircases, and bas-reliefs depicting processions and ceremonies.

Near Persepolis, in Naqsh-i-Rustam, a sanctuary from an earlier period became a burial site for Achaemenid kings. Four caves dug into the rock contained the tombs of Darius, Xerxes, Artaxerxes I and Darius II.

This bronze ornament from a sceptre represents two deer being attacked by two lions.
This example of Luristan art (800-600 B.C.) still shows the influence of steppe art.

The winged beasts with human heads that stood like guardians around imperial majesty.

A gold chalice decorated with a winged lion. It probably came from Ecbatana, fifth century B.C.

Shown here are the remains of the steps that led to the great audience room in the palace of Darius in Persepolis. To either side of the figures in the foreground is the carved image of a lion attacking a bull. This symbolized the triumph of good over evil.

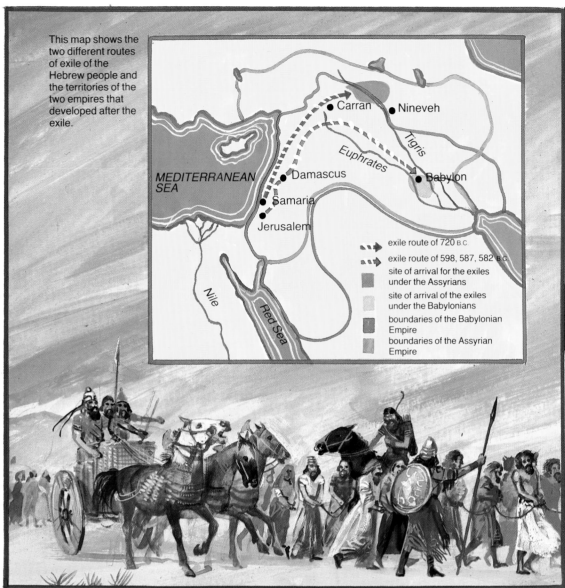

This map shows the two different routes of exile of the Hebrew people and the territories of the two empires that developed after the exile.

exile route of 720 B.C.
exile route of 598, 587, 582 B.C.
site of arrival for the exiles under the Assyrians
site of arrival of the exiles under the Babylonians
boundaries of the Babylonian Empire
boundaries of the Assyrian Empire

Above: This scene depicts the deportation of the Hebrews to Babylonia. *Top, middle:* In exile, the people adapted to daily life in a new land, but preserved their traditions and the memories of their Hebrew forefathers.

A stone carved with Babylonian deities. It comes from the twelfth century B.C.

THE EXILE AND RETURN OF THE JEWS

Israel's Exile in Assyria

When the Assyrian king Sargon II expanded the Assyrian Empire in the eighth century B.C., the conquered territory included the kingdom of Israel. Sargon then uprooted the population of Israel and sent other people to settle in the region, obliterating most of the tradition of the northern kingdom. Some of the Jews mingled with the people of their new country. Others gathered into communities that survived under the different sovereigns who ruled northern Mesopotamia. Still others went back to Palestine during the period of Persian domination.

The Exile in Babylonia

In the sixth century B.C. the Babylonians captured Judah and took many of its people prisoner. The captives, including priests, royal administrators, intellectuals, artisans and traders, were deported to Babylonia. This period came to be called the Babylonian Exile.

Once in exile, the Jews tried to make the best of their fate, in the hope that they would eventually return to their homeland. This period of exile was a time of national reflection. The people tried to understand the religious consequences of events that had forced them to choose between keeping their culture alive and separate, or mingling with the people of the new country. Unlike the people of the northern kingdom, the people of Judah chose to keep the Hebrew tradition alive.

The Hebrew Bible

During the exile in Babylonia and in the following centuries, biblical texts containing the revealed word of the God of Israel, Yahweh, took on their final form. The most ancient papyrus and leather rolls, which the priests and the scribes had salvaged from destruction, were copied. Parts of God's revelation that had been passed on orally were then written down.

The Hebrew Bible is made up of The Torah (Law), which consists of

Back in Jerusalem, the Jews rebuilt the walls and the altar, where sacrifices were again performed.

The siege of Babylon in 539 B.C. is recorded on this clay cylinder.

he five books of the Pentateuch Genesis, Exodus, Leviticus, Num-ers and Deuteronomy); the Nevim Prophets), and the Ketuvim (Books f Wisdom) which include the 'salms, the book of Job, the 'roverbs, and the Song of Songs. hese texts formed the Old Testa-nent. The early Christians accepted hem as an essential part of the evelation of God to humans and dded more books.

The prophet Ezekiel voiced the people's conflicting thoughts on this matter. Ezekiel was a priest who had been deported in his youth and had grown up in Babylon. But he dreamed of a completely different homeland from the one he had known. The new Judah would be a country without a king, centred on the Temple, and strictly abiding by the law of Moses. Under the direction of a High Priest, there would be a strict distinction between Jews and non-Jews. These principles surfaced during the period following the exile; they became the basis of the Jewish nation.

Return and Reconstruction

In 538 B.C., the Persian king Cyrus con-quered Babylonia. He then issued a decree allowing the exiled people to return to their homelands. The events after this are very vague, and no authentic historical reports exist. In the beginning, the Jewish homecom-ers, few in number, faced many difficulties.

Their old land was either uncultivated or in the hands of other peoples, and survival was not easy. They wanted to erect a new temple from the ruins of the old, but it was first necessary to build an altar for sacrifices in Jerusalem.

The first leaders of the new nation were Zerubbabel, a descendant of the family of David, and the High Priest Joshua. The prophets who inspired the rebirth of Israel were Haggai and Zechariah. Guarding the integrity of the law of Moses was the scribe Ezra. Probably between 445-443 B.C., Nehe-miah first visited Jerusalem. He was intensely involved in reconstructing Jerusalem. He was equally interested in social reform on the basis of the laws that had been written during the exile and in the hope of a rebirth of the nation of Israel. The reconstruction was tied to the personalities of their two leaders, Ezra and Nehemiah, who with Ezekiel are considered by Jews to be the architects of Judaism.

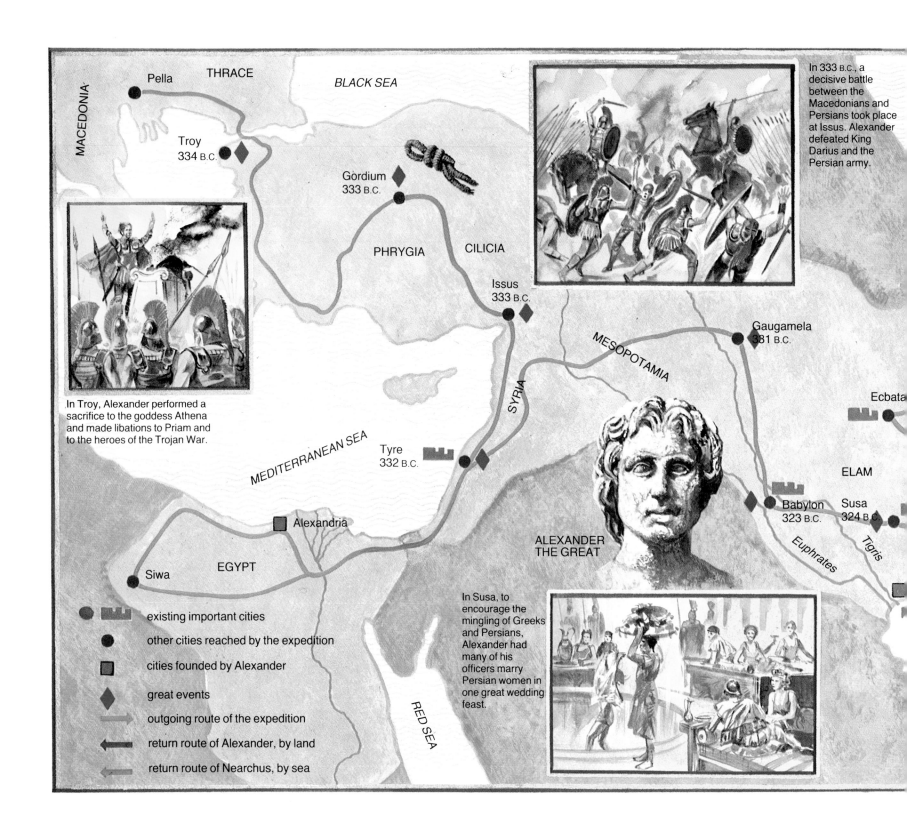

In Troy, Alexander performed a sacrifice to the goddess Athena and made libations to Priam and to the heroes of the Trojan War.

In 333 B.C., a decisive battle between the Macedonians and Persians took place at Issus. Alexander defeated King Darius and the Persian army.

ALEXANDER THE GREAT

In Susa, to encourage the mingling of Greeks and Persians, Alexander had many of his officers marry Persian women in one great wedding feast.

Map labels: Pella · THRACE · BLACK SEA · MACEDONIA · Troy 334 B.C. · Gordium 333 B.C. · PHRYGIA · CILICIA · Issus 333 B.C. · MESOPOTAMIA · Gaugamela 331 B.C. · Ecbata · Tyre 332 B.C. · MEDITERRANEAN SEA · SYRIA · ELAM · Babylon 323 B.C. · Susa 324 B.C. · Alexandria · Siwa · EGYPT · Euphrates · Tigris · RED SEA

Legend:
- existing important cities
- other cities reached by the expedition
- cities founded by Alexander
- great events
- outgoing route of the expedition
- return route of Alexander, by land
- return route of Nearchus, by sea

THE GREEKS CONQUER WESTERN ASIA

Alexander the Great Avenges the Greeks

In the fourth century B.C., the ancient hostility between Greeks and Persians erupted into a new war. This war was to lead to the fall of Persia and the entire Achaemenid Empire. For in this war, the Persians faced not only the Greeks, but also the Macedonians led by Alexander the Great. Through his campaigns, Alexander sought to revenge the Greeks, to spread Hellenistic culture throughout the east and to strengthen existing political alliances.

In 334 B.C., an army of about forty thousand men led by Alexander crossed the Hellespont and performed a sacrifice in Troy in remembrance of the Trojan War. After a few months, almost all of Asia Minor had fallen into Alexander's hands. Alexander later penetrated Syria, where in late 333 B.C. he defeated the Persian army led by the great commander Darius. With this victory, Alexander won access to the eastern coasts and Mesopotamia. The Phoenician towns were divided. Only Tyre dared to resist the conquest and eventually had to surrender after a siege of seve months.

In Egypt, Alexander founded the city o Alexandria, and visited the oracle of Ammo in Siwa. From Egypt, Alexander made his wa back to Asia. In 331 B.C., at Gauga mela Arbela, a decisive clash between Persians an Macedonians took place. Darius awaited Alex ander on terrain which was favourable to h war chariots. But once again he was defeate and forced to flee the battlefield. The capita of the empire now fell one after the othe Entering Babylon, Alexander offered a sacr fice to the god Marduk in order to become kin of the entire world. In Persepolis, Alexande

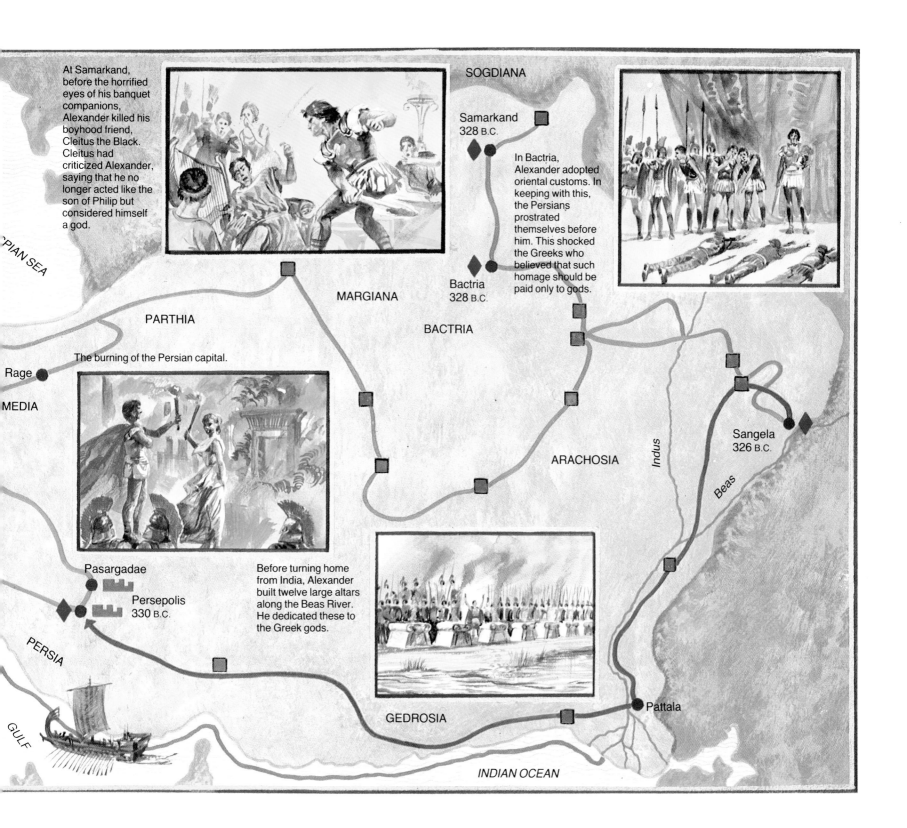

At Samarkand, before the horrified eyes of his banquet companions, Alexander killed his boyhood friend, Cleitus the Black. Cleitus had criticized Alexander, saying that he no longer acted like the son of Philip but considered himself a god.

SOGDIANA

Samarkand 328 B.C.

In Bactria, Alexander adopted oriental customs. In keeping with this, the Persians prostrated themselves before him. This shocked the Greeks who believed that such homage should be paid only to gods.

Bactria 328 B.C.

MARGIANA

PARTHIA

BACTRIA

CASPIAN SEA

The burning of the Persian capital.

Rage

MEDIA

ARACHOSIA

Indus

Sangela 326 B.C.

Beas

Pasargadae

Persepolis 330 B.C.

Before turning home from India, Alexander built twelve large altars along the Beas River. He dedicated these to the Greek gods.

PERSIA

Pattala

GEDROSIA

GULF

INDIAN OCEAN

The Conquest of the East

eized the treasure of the Persian kings and urned the city. In the summer of 330 B.C., Darius was killed by Bessus, one of his own nobles. Alexander then proclaimed himself heir to the Achaemenid Empire.

Alexander's army conquered the lands of Hyrcania, Parthia, Aria and Arachosia. Crossing the Hindu Kush mountains, he moved into Bactria and Sogdiana, where the plains of central Asia began. Alexander dreamed of reaching India, and headed south. In 326 B.C., he allied himself with the king of Taxila against Porus, an Indian prince. Again victori-

ous, he crossed the Indus River and reached one of its tributaries, the Beas River. At this point, his soldiers refused to go any farther and Alexander was compelled to turn back.

On the way home, the Macedonian army marched along the course of the Indus River for a time, then divided into two groups. Nearchus, one of Alexander's commanders, led the fleet by sea to the mouths of the Tigris and the Euphrates rivers. Alexander, with part of the army, took the more difficult route across the terrible desert of Gedrosia. The forces joined up again in Susa.

After only a few tumultuous years of war, the political ideas of Alexander changed. He

wished for the Greeks and the "barbarians" to mingle and to create a new political unity. To aid this merger, Alexander encouraged marriages between Greeks and the peoples he had conquered. He himself married the daughter of a Sogdiana noble and later three Persian princesses. In Susa, hundreds of Greek generals and soldiers married non-Greek women in a single day. For the capital of his vast empire, Alexander chose Babylon. In 323 B.C., returning there to reunite the army, Alexander suddenly fell sick with malaria. He died after a few days aged only 32. His death marked the end of one of the most incredible lives of conquest in the history of the world.

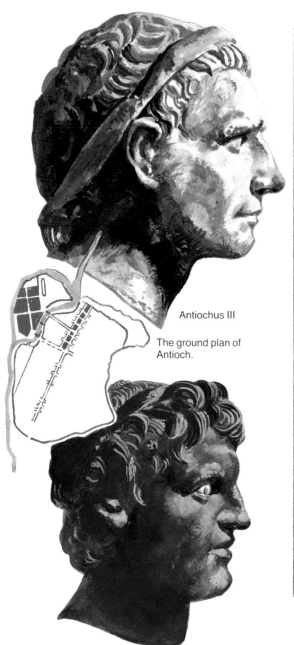

Antiochus III

The ground plan of Antioch.

A bronze head of Seleucus I, the founder of the dynasty, is pictured.

The main road of Antioch was very wide. It was built of stone slabs and had wide pavements. It was flanked by colonnades under which were numerous shops. The city's population was composed of artisans, farmers, merchants and slaves. Trade flourished. The camel was used for carrying traders' goods on long journeys. Asses were common beasts of burden in and around the city.

THE KINGDOM OF THE SELEUCIDS

The Hellenistic States

Alexander died without an appointed heir. His generals considered themselves to be his successors, and promptly began to fight over the empire. Some of the generals wished to keep Alexander's empire intact as one unit; others wanted to create independent states. In 321 B.C., the empire was effectively broken up, and its territories were assigned to be ruled by various generals.

The generals had frequent quarrels. Eventually, between 307 and 305 B.C., each general was given the title of king, and the empire was divided into separate kingdoms. Macedonia, including Greece, came under the rule of the dynasty of the Antigonids. Anatolia, Mesopotamia, Syria and the Asian lands to the east passed into the hands of the Seleucids. Egypt

was ruled by the dynasty of the Ptolemies. In all of these states, the Greek conquerors continued to rule over the local populations. These states came to be called Hellenistic states.

The Seleucids, Founders of Towns

The dynasty of the Seleucids was founded by Seleucus I Nicator, who controlled the bulk of the empire. He succeeded the Great Kings of Persia. The Seleucids added an important feature to the traditional governmental system of the Persians. They built numerous fortified towns, sending Greeks and Macedonians to populate them. All of these towns had a high degree of independence, but they were protected by a royal garrison and were under the

This statue of the city deity, Athena Tyche, dates from the third century B.C. Representing the good luck of Antioch, she sits on a rock, her head crowned by fortified walls. At her feet is the Orontes River.

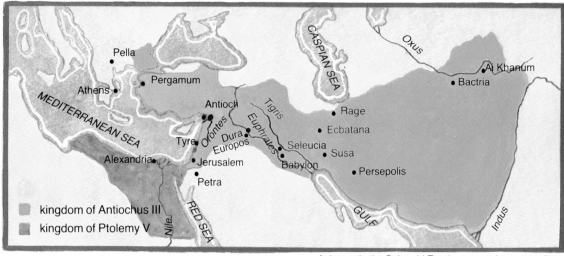

At its peak, the Seleucid Empire covered a vast territory, from the Mediterranean Sea to India.

The main temple of Ai Khanum was located in one of the Greek towns in Bactria. In the background morning mist rises from the River Oxus.

control of a governor. The Seleucid towns were great centres of Hellenistic culture. The most important of these was Antioch in Syria. Founded by Seleucus I on the banks of the Orontes River, this town became the kingdom's capital.

The economic life of the kingdom of the Seleucids was based on agricultural production and trade. The kings took special care in maintaining the network of roads that served as trade routes. These roads went from India to the ports of the Mediterranean coast.

The Loss of the East

The kingdom of the Seleucids was so vast that it was difficult to rule. By 303 B.C., the Indian territories had already been abandoned. Because of changes in the Seleucids' military, political and economic interests in the Mediterranean, managing the central and eastern parts of the empire also became impossible.

In 239 B.C., Iranian people from the steppes of central Asia invaded the territories along the Caspian Sea. These were the Parthians, against whom the Seleucids fought many wars.

Gradually, the Parthians conquered many regions of the empire. This resulted in a disruption of communication between the core of the Seleucid kingdom and its easternmost territories.

The eastern part of the empire showed increasing tendencies toward secession. At the end of the third century, the Seleucids were forced to recognize the independence of the kingdom of Bactria. This was a vast territory, stretching as far as northwest India. Still other divisions followed. The Greek-Bactrian territories developed in their own direction and continued to spread Hellenistic culture towards central Asia and India. Eventually, in 100 B.C., they were conquered by the Scythians and later by the Kushans.

The End of the Seleucid Kingdom

The gradual loss of territories to the east, and constant fights with Egypt over Syria to the west, reduced the kingdom's military strength. King Antiochus III attempted to regain the territories that had been seized by the Parthians and backed Macedonia in the

war against Rome (192-188 B.C.). But both the Parthians and the Romans, who were already present on the eastern Mediterranean, were too powerful for the Seleucids. Upon the death of Antiochus III in 187 B.C., the dynasty declined rapidly.

Hellenistic Palestine

Initially, Palestine was ruled by the Ptolemies of Egypt. In 198 B.C. it was annexed to the kingdom of Antiochus III. Under Antiochus III, the Jews were allowed to continue their cultural and religious traditions. When Antiochus IV came to power, however, he tried to force Greek culture on the Jews. Many resisted and tension grew until it burst into a war for independence. The Seleucids reacted harshly, and Antiochus IV had an altar to the god Zeus built in the Jews' Temple. A movement of political opposition began, led by a family of priests known as the Hasmoneans. In 164 B.C., one of these priests, Judas Maccabeus, seized Jerusalem, purified and rededicated the Temple, and began a period of Hasmonean rule in Palestine. The Hasmonean dynasty ruled there until deposed by the Romans in 37 B.C..

THE KINGDOM OF PERGAMUM

In Asia Minor, close to the Mediterranean, the small town of Pergamum became independent of the Seleucids in 263 B.C. At first its territory was very small, but it was located in a favourable position and was quite wealthy. The princes of Pergamum sought to expand their country, taking advantage of the constant wars that were weakening the Seleucids. Following military success, Attalus I became Pergamum's king, and by 189 B.C., most of the Seleucid territories belonged to Pergamum.

The rulers of the dynasty founded by Attalus were excellent diplomats in the Mediterranean area. They realized that the small kingdom of Pergamum, squeezed between Macedonia in Europe and the Seleucids in Asia, could never survive without support from a major power. Thus they allied themselves with Rome and were able to expand their territory. They scored several victories against the Celtic populations of northern Phrygia and they often raided that kingdom.

The City of Pergamum

Under the Attalid dynasty, Pergamum became one of the most important cities of Hellenistic times. The site where the town had developed, however, was not well suited for construction work. It was a steep rocky spur at the junction of two rivers. The architects who designed the plan for the city abandoned the classical scheme of Hellenistic towns with streets crossing at right angles. Instead, they used the terrain's natural features. Showing great skill in urban landscaping, they built a city on three levels connected by steps. The upper city, the most grand in style, developed around a double square and contained a large altar to Zeus, a library and a theatre built on the slope of the rocky outcrop.

Pergamum was also a major cultural centre, particularly under kings Attalus I and Eumemes

II when it matched the grandeur of Alexandria. The city was the meeting point for literary scholars, philosophers and artists. The extensive library, supported by the king's treasury, contained many classical Greek works.

An important technical achievement was the introduction of parchment. The word "parchment" was derived from the name of the city. This writing material was invented to challenge the Egyptian monopoly on papyrus. Parchment was made from sheep or goat skin processed in a special way and made into a sturdy roll. This new material spread rapidly through the ancient world and was still used a thousand years later in medieval Europe. Paper, invented in China almost at the same time, took much longer to reach Europe.

Pergamum and Hellenistic Art

Some of the Hellenistic world's most significant art was produced in Pergamum. Two of the best known are the statue called the *Dying Gaul* and the altar of Zeus. The statue was part of a great circular monument built in memory of the defeat of the Galatians. The altar of Zeus is the most important monument of Hellenistic culture still in existence. It was built in 190 B.C. by Antiochus III to celebrate a military victory. Such imposing size was a mark of Hellenistic art.

The construction of colossal monuments as symbols of power and strength was enthusiastically adopted by many kings in Hellenistic towns. Another feature of Hellenistic art was its realism, in both sculpture and painting. Great attention was paid to detail, features and individual differences. The artists did not shrink from showing old age, sickness, suffering and ethnic differences. The idealized themes of classical Greece were abandoned, and the favourite themes were scenes of daily life, still-lifes and landscapes.

Top: Map showing the kingdom of Pergamum at the Aegean borders of Asia in 240 (light pink) and 185 B.C. (dark pink). *Bottom:* The plan of Pergamum with the acropolis (**1**) and the gymnasium (**2**).

This statue called the *Dying Gaul* was part of a bronze group erected by King Attalus I (241-197 B.C.) in memory of his victories over the Galatians. It is famous as an example of Hellenistic art, and the respect paid to the defeated enemy is evident.

Antiochus III built the altar to Zeus to celebrate the victory over the Galatians. It is the most important monument of Hellenistic art.

sheep

stretched skin

tanned roll

written parchment

Parchment was first made in the city of Pergamum. It became a standard writing material.

The acropolis of Pergamum: **1)** Agora; **2)** altar to Zeus; **3)** market place; **4)** theatre; **5)** temple of Athena; **6)** library, partially hidden by the colonnade of the temple of Athena.

57

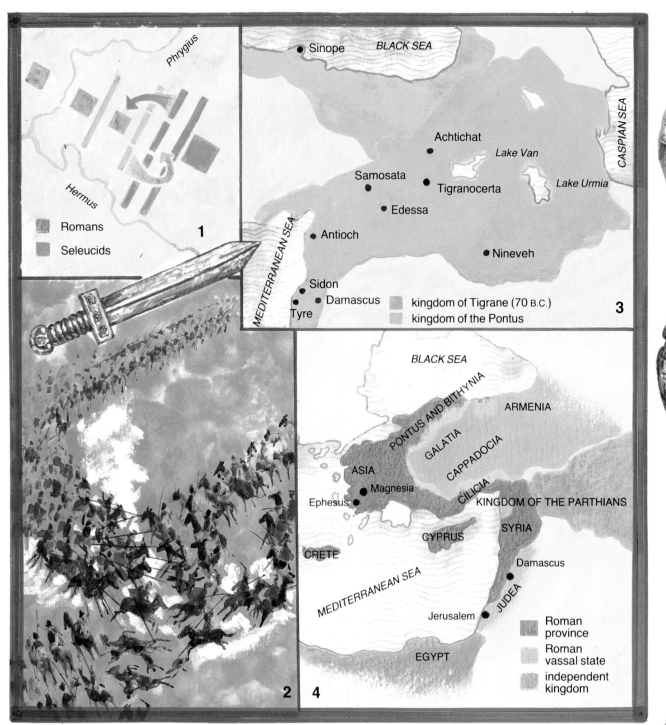

A coin bearing the head of Mithridates IV of Pontus.

Tigranes the Great is shown on this coin.

The sections above illustrate Roman expansion eastward. 1) The Battle of Magnesia, 190 B.C.. 2) This drawing shows an example of the tactics of the Roman legions. Although sometimes weak in frontal attack, the Romans succeeded in attacking the flanks of enemy formations. 3) Shaded areas on the map represent the kingdoms of Pontus and Armenia. 4) This map shows Roman expansion in Asia.

Roman cavalryman

THE ROMANS CONQUER THE EAST

Roman expansion into the eastern Mediterranean began on the Greek peninsula. The Romans had been called in to defend their allies on Italy's eastern coast. But once there, they took an offensive stance against the Macedonians in defence of the Greeks. In 196 B.C., the Romans proclaimed the liberty of the Greek cities.

By 200 B.C., Rome was on its way to becoming the strongest power in the Mediterranean, but the Seleucid Empire was still strong in Asia. The Seleucids were defeated at Thermopylae (191 B.C.), and at Magnesia (190 B.C.), and were later forced to confine themselves to Syria.

Meanwhile, the kingdom of Pergamum, allied with the Romans, was enlarged. Shrewd Roman diplomacy toward the smaller kingdoms of Asia Minor rendered them all allies of Rome. Under Rome's protection, the Armenian rulers, both north and south, declared themselves independent of the Seleucids. The next step in the Roman expansion came when King Attalus III of the independent kingdom of Pergamum died in 133 B.C. Having no heir, Attalus willed the kingdom to the Romans. In

this territory, Rome established the province of Asia Minor. Shortly afterward, Cilicia also became a Roman province.

Tigranes the Great

Around 100 B.C., the Roman advance was gravely shaken by the expansion of Armenia and by the resistance of Mithridates, the king of Pontus. Armenia, having been divided

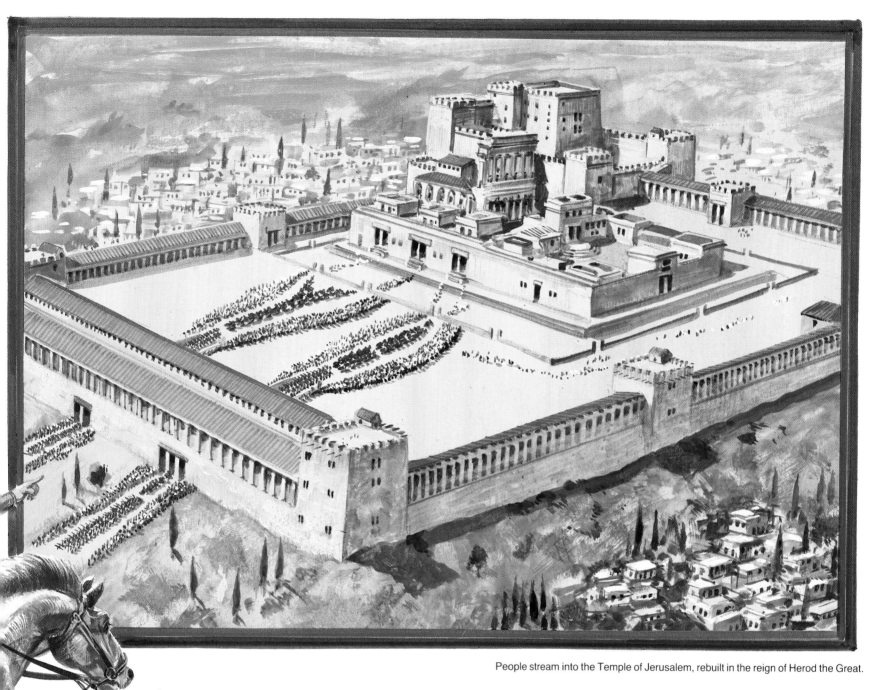

People stream into the Temple of Jerusalem, rebuilt in the reign of Herod the Great.

into two principalities, had been exposed to attacks by the Parthians. Under Tigranes the Great, however, Armenia became unified and expanded. Tigranes seized control of a Parthian province and eventually reached Mesopotamia.

In 83 B.C., some Greek cities, notably Antioch, called upon Tigranes to be the successor to the Seleucids. Tigranes' Armenian empire thus extended from the Caspian Sea to the Mediterranean Sea. His rule lasted a short time but permitted Hellenistic culture to spread more widely, with Greek settlement and new city-foundations in central Armenia.

Mithridates Challenges the Romans

Farther west, on the Black Sea, the kingdom of Pontus gained strength at the same time as Armenia was flourishing. King Mithridates Eupator took the field against the Romans. In the first war (89-85 B.C.) Mithridates occupied Rome's allied kingdoms of Bithynia and Cappadocia, then invaded Roman Asia. All of anti-Roman Greece fought with him. The Roman leader Sulla drove Mithridates from Asia and forced him to make peace.

In a second war, Mithridates was chased from Cappadocia (83-81 B.C.). In the third war (74-65 B.C.), the Romans won a decisive victory. To prepare himself for this great conflict, Mithridates had allied himself with Tigranes, the Armenian king, and had gathered an army. The Roman victory, begun by General Lucullus, was completed by Pompey the Great in 66 B.C. Mithridates committed suicide. Armenia, now defeated, returned to being a Roman protectorate. It was to remain a buffer zone between Rome and the Parthians for more than a century.

Conquest of the Hasmonean Kingdom of Palestine

Under John Hyrcanus (134-104 B.C.), one of the Hasmonean leaders after Judas Maccabeus, the Hasmonean kingdom extended itself from the confines of Judaea into a territory equal in size to the kingdom of David. But soon after, it began to decline, enmeshed in internal struggles. Rule of the Palestinian kingdom had fallen to two brothers, Aristobolus II and Hyrcanus II. The brothers turned for backing to Pompey, the Roman general who was then living in Damascus. In 63 B.C., Pompey made Aristobolus ruler of Jerusalem and victoriously entered the city and its Temple. There he named Hyrcanus II as high priest, but Palestine was reduced to little more than a Roman client-state. Under the reign of Herod, a Roman vassal, the Temple was practically rebuilt between 20 and 10 B.C.

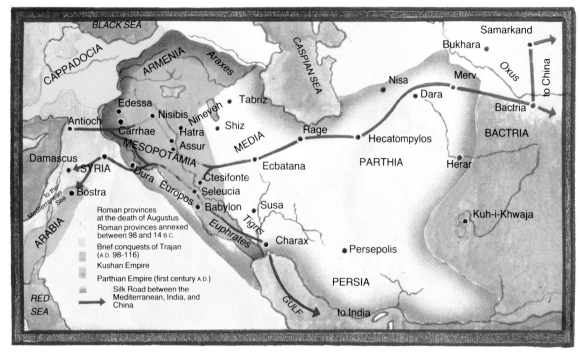

The Parthian Empire lay between the Roman Mediterranean and Kushan India.

A Parthian king grants power to a provincial governor, giving him a crown.

THE PARTHIAN EMPIRE

Around 250 B.C., nomads of Iranian origin moved out of central Asia into the territory south of the Caspian Sea. There they conquered Parthia, taking it from the Seleucid Empire, and proclaimed Arsaces, one of their own chiefs, king. From the area of their initial conquests, the Parthians, as they were called, spread themselves throughout other territories in what had been the Persian Empire. In 141 B.C., the Parthian king Mithridates I gained control of Seleucia, the great Seleucid city on the Tigris River, and proclaimed himself king of Babylon.

Conflict Over the Euphrates

Under the reign of Mithridates II (from around 123 B.C.), the Parthian Empire became a major regional power. The influence of Rome, however, was spreading from the Mediterranean towards Asia. The Euphrates River was to be, for centuries, a point of conflict between these two empires struggling for control of the Middle East.

The Roman leader Crassus, seeking a glorious victory in the east, led an expedition against the Parthians, but was disastrously defeated in the Battle of Carrhae (53 B.C.). Crassus was killed, along with more than 30,000 of his soldiers, and the Parthians captured the insignia of the Roman legions. Some thirty years later, in 20 B.C., the Roman emperor Augustus sought to make peace. Augustus obtained the return of Roman prisoners and insignias by treaty.

This statue is of a Parthian warrior in the uniform of a commander, from Hatra, second century A.D.

Parthian War Tactics

Parthian hit-and-run tactics disrupted the formations of the Roman legions. The Parthians were skilled horsemen and excellent archers. They struck effectively and then rapidly retreated to reload with fresh arrows. The "Parthian shot", as it was called, fired by an invincibly quick horseman, became famous. Toward the end of the Parthian epoch, heavy cavalry appeared, as shown in drawings from the period of armoured cavalrymen.

In a fresco from Dura Europos (first century A.D.), three people offer a sacrifice to the god Bel. The figures in the fresco are characteristic of Parthian art.

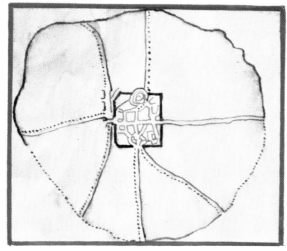

This plan was drawn for the city of Merv, which was the most important city of the region of Margiana. The city's enclosed centre remained from the Seleucid Empire and followed the model of Greek urban planning. The Parthians used it as the new city's centre and added circular walls for defence.

This head belongs to a colossal statue dedicated to the god Apollo-Mitra. It was found, together with others, among the ruins of the funerary mound of Antiochus I Commagenes at Nimrud-Dag in southern Anatolia. It dates from the first century B.C.

A century later, the Roman emperor Trajan resumed hostilities and succeeded in conquering southern Arabia, Armenia, Mesopotamia and Babylonia. Hadrian, his successor, changed Roman policy in Asia. He restored these territories to the Parthians, making the Euphrates River the boundary once again.

The Parthians and the Steppe Peoples

For the Parthian Empire, the situation was more complicated to the north and east. In these regions, they feared invasions by Iranian nomadic tribes. These tribes were moving south from the steppes and through the mountain passes of the Caucasus.

Eastward, along the border with India, the power of the Kushan Empire was growing. After having taken the Greek states of Bactria, the Kushans created a vast empire which included the Indus Valley and stretched to the Ganges Valley. The Parthians, their eyes on the west rather than the east, tried to avoid disagreements with the Kushans.

The government of the Parthian Empire maintained the established systems. Governors, or satraps, were appointed from the noble Achaemenid families. The organization of cities followed the Hellenistic tradition. The kings owned a considerable portion of the land, and governed the country through the nobility. The nobility was made up either of military officers or of local princes who raised their own armies.

The empire grew wealthy because many merchant caravans crossed its lands. One particularly important travel route had developed when the Mediterranean, under Roman rule, had become a rich market and when China had been unified under the Han dynasty. The so-called Silk Road carried silk, a precious and highly prized product, to the west.

Architecture and Art

The few Parthian cities were built with a circular plan, reminiscent of a nomadic encampment. In their building techniques, the Parthians returned to and renewed the Iranian architectural tradition. Beam roofs and colonnades were replaced with vaulted roofs.

The Parthians retained the religious and cultural traditions of the steppe nomads but were also greatly attracted to Hellenism. Until around the first century A.D., the Arsacidae dynasty (the ruling dynasty begun by Arsaces) encouraged Hellenization. One example of this Hellenization is the funeral monument to Antiochus I Commagenes at Nimrud-Dag (from the first century A.D.). On this monument, the gods are depicted in the Greek fashion. Before this, Iranian people had never shown gods in human form.

THE LIFE AND TEACHINGS OF JESUS CHRIST

During the reign of Herod in Palestine—then effectively under Roman control—an event, little noted at the time, occurred that was to change the history of the Hebrew people and the lives of many peoples and lands.

Jesus Christ, a descendant of King David, was born in the city of Bethlehem in Judaea. He was the son of a carpenter, Joseph, and his wife Mary. When Jesus was presented at the Temple for circumcision, which was a ritual among the Jews, two pious Israelites, Simeon and Anne, announced that the baby would become the Messiah. The Messiah was the descendant of David who, according to prophecy and scripture, would free the Jewish people. Until his thirtieth year, Jesus lived at Nazareth, in Galilee.

The Ministry of Jesus

In A.D. 28-29, the prophet John the Baptist began to preach along the River Jordan. In his teachings, John urged the Jews to live lives of virtue, justice and truth. John baptized many people in the waters of the Jordan, including Jesus.

After a period of fasting in the desert, Jesus started to preach. His mission was to proclaim the Kingdom of God. Jesus wanted to show the people that God was not an incomprehensible power but was the Father of all. Jesus spoke to the humble, the simple and the sick. He also knew the art of healing and cured the lame, the blind and the lepers.

The new teachings attracted more and more interest among ordinary people. Jesus had many followers. People were awed by his great humanity, by his capacity to understand and care for everyone he met, by his preaching, and by his goodness. From among these followers, Jesus chose twelve men to be his disciples and assist him. These men were called apostles.

Betrayed and Executed

Jesus' preaching and actions alarmed the two most powerful groups of Jews: the Pharisees and the Sadducees. The Pharisees feared that Jesus' teachings would change religious practices. The Sadducees feared that Jesus' popularity would lead to political disorder. Some of his followers, including the apostles, insisted that Jesus had come to free Israel from

Accompanied by his disciples, Jesus preaches to the people.

the Roman Empire, though he himself denied the charge.

In the spring of A.D. 30 or 33, Jesus arrived in Jerusalem to celebrate the Passover, the Jewish festival celebrating their liberation from Egypt. Jesus was welcomed by the people of the city, who saluted him as their king, the Messiah. He preached in the Temple and celebrated with his disciples.

Betrayed by one of his disciples, Judas, Jesus was arrested and taken before the Jewish high priests. These leaders questioned him, asking him if he was the Son of God. When Jesus did not deny this, the leaders accused him of having blasphemed. They then took him to Pontius Pilate, the Roman governor. The high priests told Pilate that Jesus had claimed he was the King of the Jews. At their urging, Pilate sentenced Jesus to death by crucifixion.

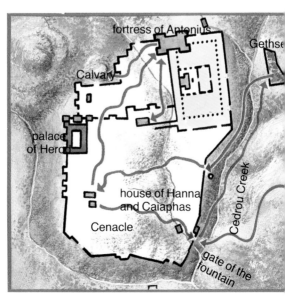

Map showing the path of Jesus to Jerusalem during the last days of his earthly life.

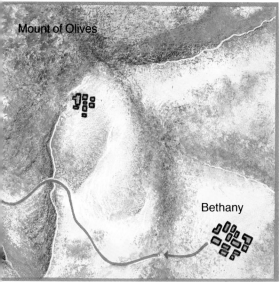

Mount of Olives

Bethany

The Resurrection

Christians believe that Jesus rose from the dead three days after his crucifixion. The celebration of his resurrection is known as Easter Sunday. Accounts of the resurrection come from the testimony of Jesus' disciples as recorded in the Gospels. Doubtful at first, the apostles themselves were convinced of the event only through meetings with the resurrected Christ. The Gospels tell how one of Jesus' followers, Mary Magdalene, discovered his empty tomb. The writings also relate several appearances of Jesus to the apostles and his ascension into heaven. The death and resurrection of Jesus lay at the heart of a new religion: Christianity.

The New Testament

The texts of the Bible that describe Jesus' life and the beginning of the Christian community are called the New Testament. Jesus did not record his own teachings, many of which were related in the form of parables. These, like the story of his life, were later written down by his disciples. Nearly all our knowledge of the events of Jesus' life comes from four short books within the New Testament. The books are called the Gospels, which means good news. They were written by Matthew, Mark, Luke and John.

Other writings of the New Testament include the Acts of the Apostles and the Epistles (letters). In the Acts of the Apostles, Luke recounts how the early church was created, as the first Christian communities were founded, by travelling teachers such as Paul. Tradition attributes fourteen of the Epistles to Paul. Scholars are certain that Paul wrote five or six of these letters, but recognize that the others may not have been his work. Three other letters, as well as Revelation, are attributed to the apostle John. Finally, two epistles were written by Peter, one by James, and one by Jude. All of these texts were written in the second half of the first century A.D.

The round market place in Gerasa, characterized by four groups of four columns built in the third century A.D.

THE EASTERN EMPERORS AND ROMANIZATION

Asia was a land of ancient civilizations, rich in political organization and urban life long before the Romans arrived. The Romans undertook the task of ruling this refined world with respect and caution. After gaining control of a territory, they were tolerant of local customs. They allowed Greek towns to retain formal freedom and, especially from the second century A.D. on, they encouraged people from the eastern regions to become members of the senate and of the government of the empire.

This effort was well rewarded. It helped to merge the eastern Hellenistic and Roman traditions. People from the east were at ease in the Roman Empire. Even when the western part of the empire was lost to the barbarians, the east remained faithful to Rome.

The political integration of Asia with Rome reached its height in the third century. At that

time, Julia Domna, who belonged to the royal dynasty of the priests of the sun god of Emesa, in Syria, married Septimius Severus, who became the Roman emperor. Their offspring, from Caracalla to Severus Alexander, were to rule the empire (A.D. 211-235). Later on, Philip the Arab became emperor. Of Arabian descent, Philip is considered by some to be the first Christian emperor.

Philip II the Arab

Cultural Exchanges

The Romans were true protectors of Hellenism. They so admired the Greek culture that they invited Greek artists to come to Italy. They also brought large quantities of art from the Orient to decorate their towns and homes. This artistic and cultural influx transformed the Roman world, making it more sophisticated and cosmopolitan. Thanks to these exchanges, some Greek ideas, such as the philo-

sophy of Stoicism, also took root in Rome.

Despite Roman influence, the original Hellenistic culture remained vigorous. The Greek language remained predominant, but from the third century, local languages began to reappear. In the fine arts, especially in architecture, Roman patterns and styles were used side by side with those from the east. As

The city of Miletus probably looked like this in Roman times.

Miletus

Rhodes

Antioch

Palmira

Baalbek

Berytos

Gerasa

Petra

MEDITERRANEAN SEA

Left: Remains of the arch and column-flanked road in Palmira are shown. This ancient oasis in the Syrian Desert reached its spendour in the third century A.D. in the Roman epoch.

Right: The central court in the acropolis of Baalbek is seen in detail. The acropolis was a large Roman architectural complex. *Lower right:* The Romans made this city into an Arabic province in A.D. 106.

The archaeological remains of the temple of Mithras were found in Dura Europos.

The map shows some of the important Asian cities of the Roman Empire.

The Cult of Mithras

Mithras, god of the sun, was of Iranian origin. Mithras was the protector god of the Parthian sovereigns. Impressed no doubt by the Parthians' success in war, Roman soldiers adopted Mithras. Soldiers of the Roman army spread the cult from Mesopotamia to all the provinces of the Roman Empire.

According to mythology, the sun ordered Mithras to kill the primeval bull. Mithras obeyed. The bull's death set the creation of the world in motion. After the task was complete, Mithras and the sun feasted. This feast was re-enacted by Mithras's worshippers.

Mithras was honoured by the emperors of the third century A.D., especially Aurelian.

seen in the great monuments of Petra, Gerasa, Palmira, and Baalbek, the proportions of the buildings changed. Straight lines gave way to broken ones, and curved surfaces appeared.

Within the Roman Empire, Asia stood out for its incredible wealth. The level of prosperity in the eastern territories, Syria in particular, was unmatched. Along the Silk Road, precious silks were brought to the Mediterranean coast. Silk had been invented in China, which held a monopoly over it. Silk had been highly sought after in Rome since its appearance at the beginning of the Christian Era. Other major factors which contributed to the development and well-being of the eastern territories were their large and industrious populations and their specialized agriculture.

Religious Fervour

Rome was influenced by religious developments in the East. When Christianity spread throughout Asia Minor, it stimulated the older religions to new growth. This sudden religious fervour seems to have struck a chord in the hearts of people in many lands. Within a short period of time, the eastern empire was a vital religious centre. This vitality seeped into Italy and into the western part of the empire, mainly through the army. Priests and followers of numerous diverse cults were found throughout the empire. Among the most important cults was that of Mithras, god of the sun.

Hunting was one of the favourite sports of Sassanian sovereigns and nobles. This picture shows Sassanians hunting boar in a swamp, using elephants and boats.

Roman Empire under Diocletian, fourth century A.D.

Kushan Empire

Sassanian Empire, fourth century A.D.

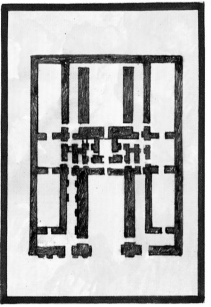

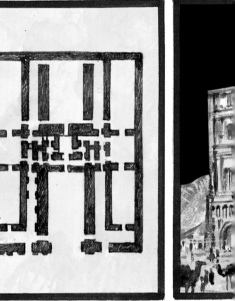

Shown above is the ground plan of the palace of Ctesiphon. The palace (above right) was built in the third century A.D. The huge, arched entrance led to the huge *ivan*, which was a three-sided room without windows.

THE SASSANIANS

The kingdom of the Parthians was shaken by violent civil wars during the last years of its existence. In A.D. 227 Ardashir, prince of the small province of Perside, collected all of his forces and defeated the last king of the Parthian dynasty. The new sovereigns were called Sassanians after Ardashir's grandfather, Sassan. The Sassanians came from a region in the heart of Iran and appeared to be the restorers of the old Persian national and religious traditions.

The Sassanians, like the Parthians, were kept busy defending their territory. To the east, they had to deal with the steppe peoples; to the west the Roman Empire was a source of trouble. But the Sassanians were not willing to give up any territory to Rome. In fact, they conquered some Roman land and established the border between the two empires along the Euphrates River. Wars between Romans and Sassanians were frequent in the third century.

A catastrophic setback for the Romans occurred when the Sassanian king Shapur I defeated the Roman emperor Valerian. Valerian was taken prisoner in A.D. 260.

Sassanian Society

The Sassanians were innovators in the organization of government. Under the sovereign, officials were responsible for individual provinces. This system made it possible to keep the country united. Additionally, people from all social classes served in the army. The nobles formed the armoured cavalry, farmers formed the infantry, and skilled auxiliary soldiers were hired from neighbouring nations.

In social life, the importance of the nobility increased. The rulers did not want to be controlled by the ancient noble Achaemenid families, so they constantly created new nobles. Sassanian society can be imagined as a series of concentric circles. At the centre was the king with his court, around them being the great families of the Achaemenid tradition. Within the next ring were nobles who had reached this status in recent times, followed by the small landowners. These landowners, or free men, had the task of collecting taxes in their territory. Forming the last, and largest circle were farmers and shepherds.

Religion

Under the Sassanians, Zoroaster's religion, Zoroastrianism, became the state religion. The Magi, an ancient caste of priests who performed the sacrifices, also accepted the doctrine of Zoroaster. However, the Sassanian Empire was not exempt from the influence of

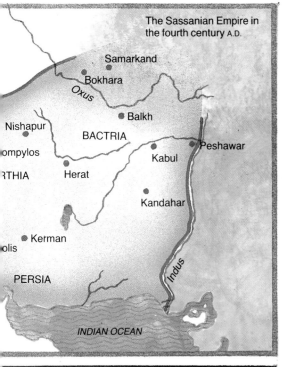

The Sassanian Empire in the fourth century A.D.

Samarkand
Bokhara
Oxus
Balkh
Nishapur
BACTRIA
Peshawar
ompylos
Kabul
Herat
RTHIA
Kandahar
Kerman
olis
PERSIA
Indus
INDIAN OCEAN

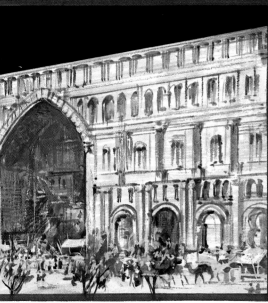

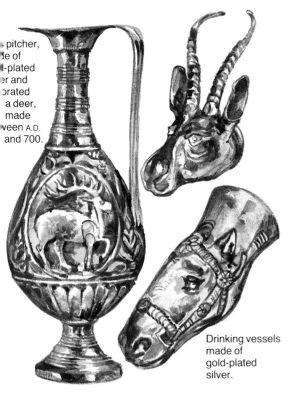

pitcher, ... of ...-plated ... and ...orated ... a deer, ... made ...een A.D. ... and 700.

Drinking vessels made of gold-plated silver.

The Sassanian king Shapur I accepts the surrender of a Roman emperor. The illustration is taken from a rock bas-relief in Naqsh-i-Rustam, from the third century A.D.

Mani and Manicheism

Mani was a great religious figure. He was born in Ctesiphon in A.D. 216, and grew up in an environment of Judaic-Christian fervour. He experienced two divine revelations, knew Indian mysticism, and for a certain period was allowed to preach in public. But during the rule of the Sassanian king Bahram I, the Magi accused Mani of leading the people away from the official religion. Under pressure, the king sentenced Mani to death. Mani died after twenty-six days of torture.

The basic principles of Manicheism are contained in a book written by Mani himself. Through them, Manicheism offered a path to salvation. His book preached that God was the highest good and that creation was the work of the Prince of Darkness who sought to gain possession of the light of God. Human beings have light within them, but this light is imprisoned inside the bodily matter. Through knowledge, it is possible to escape from the prison of life, nature and existence, thus returning the light to God and destroying the world. This religious ideal believed in a final victory for God, at the expense of life, nature, the world and the body, all of which were considered expressions of evil.

contemporary eastern religions. Other cults, such as that of fire, continued to be followed, and new religions were introduced.

Art

In Ctesiphon, a city of Parthian origin, Shapur I built a magnificent palace. At the front of the palace was an *ivan*, which was a huge, three-sided, windowless room. The fourth side opened to the outside through a pointed arch.

The Sassanians learned a great deal about city-building from Roman prisoners and from other foreign workers who were summoned to build the Sassanian towns. They often abandoned the traditional circular plan of the Parthian towns, replacing it with Hellenistic plans that arranged streets at right angles.

A typical form of Sassanian art was the bas-relief stone sculpture. Sovereigns used sculpture to celebrate their dynasty and their military victories. The Sassanians' skill in reproducing human and animal shapes was later expressed in jewellery, in patterns on fabric, and in objects of daily use.

The apostle Paul

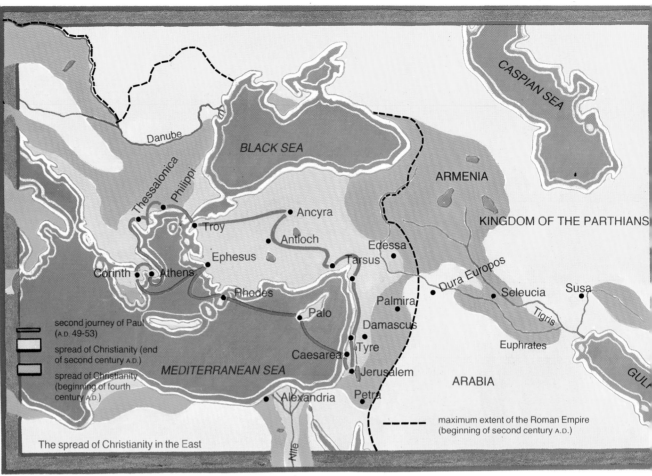

The spread of Christianity in the East

second journey of Paul (A.D. 49-53)

spread of Christianity (end of second century A.D.)

spread of Christianity (beginning of fourth century A.D.)

- - - - maximum extent of the Roman Empire (beginning of second century A.D.)

THE SPREAD OF CHRISTIANITY

The name *christianoi* appeared for the first time among the people of Antioch. The word indicated the followers of the new faith—the first of whom were Jews. In the first Christian communities, people shared their possessions, lived a life of intense prayer and met in private homes. Soon the Jews questioned whether it was possible for non-Jews (called Gentiles) to share in the Christian communities. In the Council of Jerusalem, the disciples Peter and Paul confronted one another on this issue. Paul's view that Gentiles could be converted to the new religion was accepted. This decision permitted the spread of Christianity throughout the world.

Paul's Missions

Paul (Saul) was a Jew who had converted to Christianity. He became very active in missionary work and contributed greatly to the early spread of Christianity. He preached mainly to Gentiles. Paul believed that Christianity was a religion for all human beings, and therefore nobody had the right to limit its spread. In his four journeys, Paul reached Syria and the coastal towns of Asia Minor,

Above is an illustration of the christening chapel of Dura Europos on the Euphrates River. It is the most ancient Christian church known and was built at the end of the third century.

Macedonia and Greece. In many towns, his preaching resulted in the formation of Christian communities, with which Paul kept in touch by letter. In his last journey, Paul travelled to Rome, where he preached for two years. According to tradition, he died with Peter during the persecution of Nero in A.D. 67.

The Church Organizes

Towards the end of the second century A.D., Christianity began to spread throughout the Mediterranean region and flourished in the eastern regions. The persecutions of the second century did not seriously hinder this

expansion. In the third century, the periods of peace became longer, and when crisis struck the Roman Empire, the Christians' belief proved much more resilient amid disaster than the beliefs of other cults and religions in the East.

The Church began to organize itself. Bishops were appointed to supervise the local religious leaders, or clergy. Churches were built, and Christianity spread beyond the empire's borders. It was brought to Persia first by missionaries and later by prisoners of the Sassanian kings.

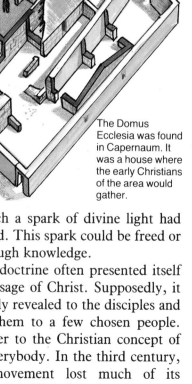

The apostle Peter

Travelling missionaries visit Christians in a Syrian village.

The Domus Ecclesia was found in Capernaum. It was a house where the early Christians of the area would gather.

War in Palestine

In the first century A.D., the political situation in Palestine worsened. Bad leadership had exasperated the population. Among the Jews, the most eager revolutionaries were the Zealots. The Zealots wanted to use force to free the Jews from tyranny. In A.D. 66, war broke out. The Romans, at first expelled, slowly regained territory under the leadership of Vespasian and his son, Titus.

In the spring of A.D. 70, the final siege of Jerusalem began. It lasted for five months, with great sufferings on the part of the people now tyrannized by the Zealots. The Temple, which

was also a fortress, was eventually set on fire and destroyed in A.D. 70. In September, the city was razed, and the Jewish people were sold as slaves.

At this point, the paths of Judaism and Christianity divided. With the destruction of the Temple, the Jews were deprived of their most sacred religious sacrificial site. They were left with only prayer and religious education. Their hopes for an apocalypse and the coming of a Messiah remained unfulfilled, and the teaching of the Pharisees became predominant.

Christianity and Greek Culture

In the Middle East, Christianity had to come to terms with Greek philosophical thought. To pre-Christian thinkers, Christian ideas such as the incarnation of God as man were inconceivable. This prompted numerous attacks on Christianity. Christian writers called Apologists tried to defend the new religion and explain the Christian viewpoint. Some writers considered Greek culture to be unimportant because it was connected to paganism. Others argued that Christianity could complete and inform pagan culture.

The debate continued through the second and third centuries. The more the Christians tried to explain the novelty of Christ's message, the more they blended in Greek philosophy. This philosophy offered great possibilities for further investigation. It also used a language which was understood by all the human beings of the time.

The Hellenistic world teemed with religions, cults and teachings which greatly influenced Christians. All of these currents are referred to by the name of *gnosis*, a Greek word meaning "knowledge". The Gnostics believed that the world was dominated by evil forces and that the human body was composed of evil

matter, in which a spark of divine light had been imprisoned. This spark could be freed or saved only through knowledge.

The Gnostic doctrine often presented itself as the true message of Christ. Supposedly, it had been secretly revealed to the disciples and passed on by them to a few chosen people. This ran counter to the Christian concept of salvation for everybody. In the third century, the Gnostic movement lost much of its strength, while the Christian churches were able to reaffirm their positive vision of the world. This trend was confirmed in A.D. 313, when Emperor Constantine granted tolerance to the Church throughout the Roman Empire.

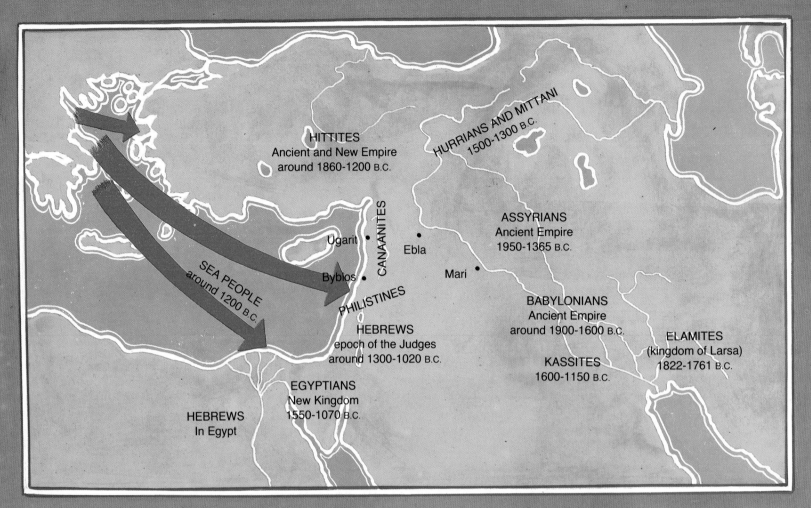

Map 1. The ascendancy of Babylonians and Hittites occurred around 2000-1200 B.C.

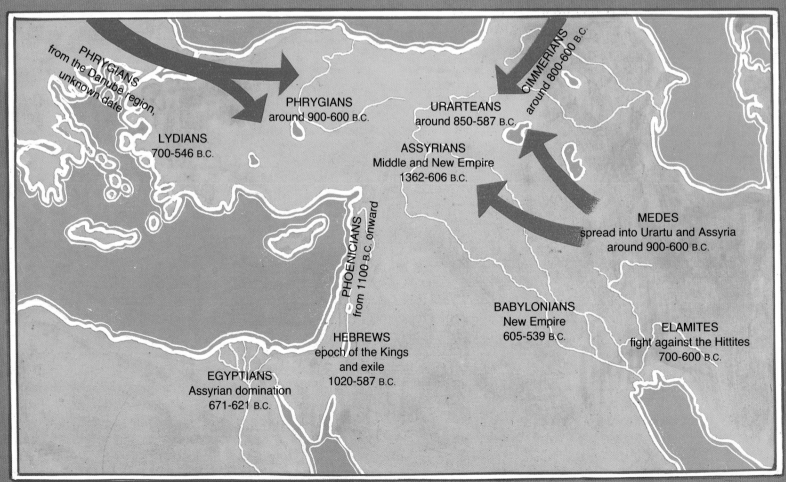

Map 2. In the period 1100 539 B.C. the Assyrians and New Babylonians were dominant forces in the Middle East.

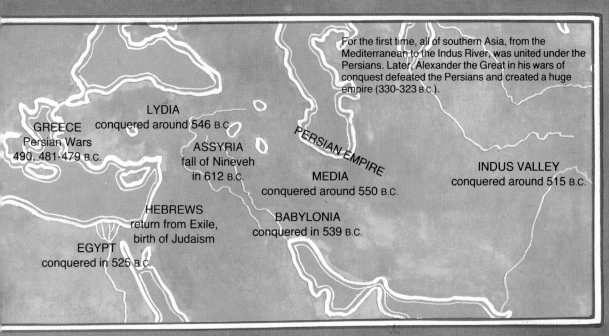

For the first time, all of southern Asia, from the Mediterranean to the Indus River, was united under the Persians. Later, Alexander the Great in his wars of conquest defeated the Persians and created a huge empire (330-323 B.C.).

GREECE
Persian Wars
490, 481-479 B.C.

LYDIA
conquered around 546 B.C.

ASSYRIA
fall of Nineveh
in 612 B.C.

PERSIAN EMPIRE

MEDIA
conquered around 550 B.C.

INDUS VALLEY
conquered around 515 B.C.

HEBREWS
return from Exile,
birth of Judaism

BABYLONIA
conquered in 539 B.C.

EGYPT
conquered in 525 B.C.

Map 3. The Persian Empire and the Persian conquests around 600-330 B.C..

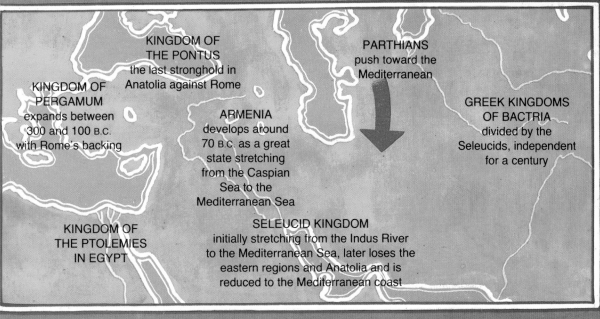

KINGDOM OF
THE PONTUS
the last stronghold in
Anatolia against Rome

PARTHIANS
push toward the
Mediterranean

KINGDOM OF
PERGAMUM
expands between
300 and 100 B.C.
with Rome's backing

ARMENIA
develops around
70 B.C. as a great
state stretching
from the Caspian
Sea to the
Mediterranean Sea

GREEK KINGDOMS
OF BACTRIA
divided by the
Seleucids, independent
for a century

KINGDOM OF
THE PTOLEMIES
IN EGYPT

SELEUCID KINGDOM
initially stretching from the Indus River
to the Mediterranean Sea, later loses the
eastern regions and Anatolia and is
reduced to the Mediterranean coast

Map 4. Hellenism (Greek-influenced culture) spread over a wide area. The Seleucids and Parthians were powerful at this time (323-63 B.C.)

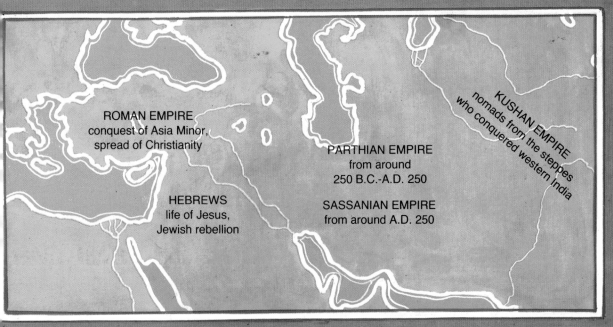

ROMAN EMPIRE
conquest of Asia Minor,
spread of Christianity

KUSHAN EMPIRE
nomads from the steppes
who conquered western India

PARTHIAN EMPIRE
from around
250 B.C.-A.D. 250

HEBREWS
life of Jesus,
Jewish rebellion

SASSANIAN EMPIRE
from around A.D. 250

Map 5. The Roman, Parthian and Sassanian empires (63 B.C.-around A.D. 300)

GLOSSARY

abolish: to do away with or destroy; to get rid of.

acropolis: Greek for the "upper part of a town"; a fortified hilltop position in ancient cities; the most famous acropolis is the one in Athens, Greece.

agriculture: the processes and activities associated with farming; the work of planting seeds, producing crops and raising animals.

animal husbandry: an occupation which involves breeding and caring for domesticated animals.

architecture: the process or profession of designing buildings of all types.

archive: a special building or place where public records and official documents are housed.

arid: dry; devoid of moisture or humidity.

aristocracy: nobility, an elite class of people who are usually rich and powerful.

artefact: any object made or crafted by human hands.

artisan: a skilled worker such as a potter or metalworker. Such skills were widespread in the Ancient Mediterranean and Asian worlds.

astronomy: the study of the stars and planets.

Avesta: the sacred religious texts of the ancient Persians.

bas-relief: a piece of sculpture in which the figures are just barely raised from a flat background.

caravan: a group of people travelling together through a desert.

catastrophe: a terrible or terrifying occurrence; a tragedy or disaster.

cavalry: troops mounted on horses; heavy cavalry wore metal armour.

ceramics: objects made of clay that are moulded into shape and baked in an oven.

chalice: a cup or goblet, frequently used in religious rites or ceremonies.

chariot: a two-wheeled horse-drawn vehicle. War chariots carried two or three fighting men.

citadel: a fortress or place of safety.

commerce: the process of buying, selling, and trading goods between one group or community and another.

continent: one of the principal land masses of the earth. Africa, Antarctica, Asia, Europe, North America, South America and Australia are continents.

cult: a specific type of religious worship, attended by its own particular rules and ceremonies.

cultivate: to prepare land for the planting and growing of crops.

cuneiform: wedge-shaped symbols used in ancient Akkadian and Sumerian inscriptions.

deity: a god; a being who possesses a divine nature.

domestication: the process of taming wild animals and then using them to pull ploughs or carts or carry goods.

dromedary: a camel with one hump. Dromedaries are used for transportation in the desert.

dynasty: a family of rulers; the period of time during which a specific family is in power. Zoser was the founder of Egypt's third dynasty.

edict: an official rule or proclamation.

emigrate: to leave one country or environment in order to settle in another.

ensi: during the Sumerian period, men who were priests as well as princes.

environment: the circumstances or conditions of a plant or animal's surroundings. The physical and social conditions of an organism's environment influence its growth and development.

epic: a long, narrative poem which relates heroic adventures or tales of a great nation.

epilogue: a final segment or closing speech added to the natural end of a book or play, which helps to provide further information or analysis.

epoch: an important, often lengthy, period in history.

excavate: to make a hole or cavity in by digging; to uncover or expose by digging. Archaeologists excavate by uncovering the buried remains of ancient towns, forts, walls, etc.

expedition: a journey or exploratory mission undertaken in order to achieve a specific purpose.

fertile: rich in natural resources; able to produce or reproduce.

frieze: decorations placed to form a border around a room or building.

hostile: having the qualities or characteristics of an enemy; unfriendly.

hypothesis: a theory based on available supporting evidence.

infantry: soldiers who are trained to fight on foot; foot-soldiers.

irrigation: carrying or delivering water to dry land by artificial means such as tunnels or ditches.

javelin: a spear-like weapon, used mainly for throwing at an advancing enemy.

kaunakes: short skirts made of fur or sheep's wool, which were the common clothes of the ancient Sumerians.

lapis lazuli: a blue gemstone highly prized for jewellery and decorating armour in ancient times.

legion: Roman army military formation; numbering 4,000 to 6,000 men; most were foot-soldiers.

liberate: to set free or release from bondage.

lunar: having to do with the moon and its changing phases.

lute: a stringed instrument much like a guitar which was used in ancient times.

lyre: a small harp-like instrument used in ancient cultures to provide musical entertainment.

Mesopotamia: an ancient country in Southwest Asia which was between the Tigris and Euphrates rivers. Modern-day Iraq covers part of ancient Mesopotamia.

migrate: to move from place to place in search of food and shelter. Migration usually revolves around seasonal changes.

monarch: the chief ruler of a state or kingdom, such as a king or queen.

Nebuchadrezzar: King of New Babylonia (reigned 605-562 B.C.). The reign of Nebuchadrezzar marked the peak of the New Babylonian empire.

nomad: a member of a tribe or people having no permanent home, but roaming about constantly in search of grazing for their herds of goats, sheep, horses, etc.

oasis: small reservoir of water in a desert, which allows the growth of trees and other plants.

obsidian: a type of gemstone which is glassy, hard and dark in colour.

oracle: any person who is believed to be capable of speaking to or communicating with the gods.

pagan: a person who does not have any system of religious belief or worship.

pankus: an assembly of warriors and noblemen during the ancient Hittite rule who helped the king determine political procedure.

papyrus: a type of parchment or paper made from a plant which grew along the Nile River during the time of the Ancient Egyptians.

peninsula: a piece of land surrounded by water on all sides, except for a narrow strip which connects it to the mainland.

plateau: an elevated and more or less level expanse of land.

polytheism: belief in the existence of more than one god, or many gods.

portico: a porch or covered walkway.

primitive: of or existing in the beginning or earliest times; ancient.

prologue: an introduction; the first part or portion of a literary work, used as preparation for what will follow.

ritual: a system of ceremonies or procedures, especially with regard to religious worship.

sanctuary: a place of peace or safety; a haven or place of rest; a special building set aside for holy worship.

Sanskrit: the ancient, formal language of old India, dating from the fourth century B.C. and still used by Buddhists today.

satraps: the rulers or protectors of individual provinces in ancient Persia.

scribe: a professional writer, manuscript copier, or keeper of written records.

scythe: a long, curved blade set into a handle used to cut grass or grain.

seal: stamp, medallion or similar object, bearing a ruler's image or mark; stamped in wax or clay as a means of identification, like a signature on a letter today.

Semitic: an adjective used to connote both languages and peoples. Semitic languages are mainly from the Middle East. Semitic peoples (named after Shem, a son of Noah) include Jews, Arabs, Babylonians, Assyrians and Phoenicians.

species: a specific type or class of plant or animal. Plant and animal species are usually very similar and can therefore interbreed only among themselves.

stele: slab or pillar of stone, carved with inscriptions; a monument.

steppe: any of the great plains of southeastern Europe and Asia, having few trees.

subjugate: to conquer and force into servitude or slavery.

subterranean: living or existing below the surface of the earth.

theocracy: a type of government in which the church has priority over and rules the state.

tributary: a small river or stream which usually flows into and is eventually part of a large one.

urban: having to do with the city or city life.

vassal: a servant or slave.

ziggurat: pyramid-like temples with stepped sides, built during the Sumerian empire.

INDEX

El-Elat, 28
Euphrates River, 7
Exodus, 31
Ezekiel, 50-51
Ezra, 51
fertile crescent, 7

G

Gnostics, 69
Gospels, 63
government
    Akkadian, 19
    Hittite, 25
    Persian, 47
grains, 8, 9
graves, 13
Greeks, 52
Gudea, 18, 19
Gutans, 18

H

Hadrian, 61
Halaf, 10
Hammurabi, 22, 23, 26
Hasmonean kingdom, 59
Hassuna, 10
Hellenism, 64
Hellenistic states, 54
Heraclidae dynasty, 38
Herodotus, 28, 38
Hezekiah, 41
Hittite Empire, 24-25, 38
Hittites, 23, 30
Hosea, 41
houses, 13
Hurrians, 25, 30

I

India, 53
irrigation, 10, 12, 15
Isaac, 30
Isin, 22
Ismael, 30
Israel, 30-31, 40-41, 50

J

Jacob, 30-31
Jehu, 41
Jerusalem, 40, 42, 51
Jesus, 62-63
John the Baptist, 62
Joram, 41
Joshua, 31
Josiah, 41
Judah, 40-41, 50, 51
Judaic War, 69
Judaism, 51, 55
judges, 31

K

kings, Babylonian, 42
kings, Hebrew, 40
Kish, 16
Kushan Empire, 61

L

Labarna, 24
Lagash, 16, 19
Lagash dynasty, 16
language
    Assyrian, 34
    Hebrew, 41
    Hurrian, 36
    Indo-European, 25
    Lycian, 38
    Persian, 46
Larsa, 22
Levantine Orient, 6
literature
    Assyrian, 34
    Babylonian, 22-23
Lugalzaggesi, 16
Lycians, 38
Lydia, 38

M

Macedonians, 52
Manasseh, 41
Mani, 67
Mari, 26
Medes, 44